DISCARD

```
LB
2343      Healy
.H35      Career counseling
1974      in the community
          college
```

CAREER COUNSELING IN THE COMMUNITY COLLEGE

The material in this publication was prepared pursuant to a contract with the National Institute of Education, U.S. Department of Health, Education and Welfare. Contractors undertaking such projects under government sponsorship are encouraged to express freely their judgments in professional and technical matters. Prior to publication, the manuscript was submitted to the ERIC Junior College Clearinghouse for critical review and determination of professional competence. This publication has met such standards. Points of view or opinions, however, do not necessarily represent the official view or opinions of either the ERIC Junior College Clearinghouse or the National Institute of Education.

Career Counseling in the Community College

By

CHARLES HEALY, Ph.D.
Assistant Professor
University of California
Los Angeles, California

CHARLES C THOMAS · PUBLISHER
Springfield · Illinois · U.S.A.

Published and Distributed Throughout the World by
CHARLES C THOMAS • PUBLISHER
Bannerstone House
301-327 East Lawrence Avenue, Springfield, Illinois, U.S.A.

ISBN 0-398-03096-0 (cloth)
ISBN 0-398-03097-9 (paper)
Library of Congress Catalog Card Number: 73-20424

With THOMAS BOOKS *careful attention is given to all details of manufacturing and design. It is the Publisher's desire to present books that are satisfactory as to their physical qualities and artistic possibilities and appropriate for their particular use.* THOMAS BOOKS *will be true to those laws of quality that assure a good name and good will.*

Printed in the United States of America
W-2

Library of Congress Cataloging in Publication Data
Healy, Charles C

    Career counseling in the community college.

    Bibliography: p.
    1. Personnel service in higher education.
2. Vocational guidance. I. Title.
LB2343.H35 1974   378.1'94'25   73-20424
ISBN 0-398-03096-0
ISBN 0-398-03097-9 (pbk.)

PREFACE

THIS BOOK DESCRIBES replicable career counseling procedures which can be learned through preservice or inservice training. Counselors should be able to respond to the career development needs of diverse clients and require, therefore, alternative procedures for facilitating career development. This book presents several alternatives approaches in a manner which will help counselors to learn these procedures and to eventually design their own.

The book began as a search for replicable career counseling procedures appropriate for the wide range of adolescents and adults in community colleges. The author and his research assistants, Ann Fogel and Betty Johnson, reviewed the professional literature, surveyed 200 community college counseling centers, and held a meeting for 55 Southern California community college counselors at UCLA in 1972. Counselors were interested in the undertaking as witnessed by the 55 percent rate of return on the survey and the good attendance at the UCLA conference. However, responses to the survey and the conference suggested that only Ulster Community College was regularly using a replicable procedure. Counselors in other colleges could duplicate parts of their counseling but not the entire process. Moreover, it became clear that although counseling researchers have been urging development of replicable procedures for years, no one had defined what constituted such a process.

The first step in organizing the book, therefore, was to define replicable counseling and specify the essential characteristics. The author then reviewed the career counseling procedures which had been located and selected thirteen which lent themselves to duplication. These procedures, many of which are new and relatively unknown to the counselor, are described in detail in this book.

However, counselors will find that even the procedures with which they are familiar—the trait factor and client-centered procedures—have been presented in a new manner, one which facilitates replicability.

CHARLES HEALY

INTRODUCTION

RAPID ADVANCES IN technology and changing mores have led increasing numbers of Americans to be concerned about their own careers and the careers of their children. Persons of all ages and circumstances face important career callings, and national leaders and educators alike are questioning the adequacy of our services for facilitating career development. Some have contended that our entire educational system needs revision and have taken steps, under the framework of the Career Education Movement, to revise the system. Others, through the newly organized National Institute of Education, are searching for the causes of career dissatisfaction through research.

Prominent among educational groups searching for solutions to America's career concerns is the guidance profession. Its members have taken career information resources from school and agency libraries to public gathering places, have recruited community people to be peer counselors and aids—expanding the potential for person-to-person career guidance, have introduced classes in career planning and decision making into many community colleges and adult education programs, have developed simulation materials to enable people to better understand the nature of occupations, and have integrated films, video and audio tapes, and computers into their programs to quickly provide people with the accurate occupational information they want.

This innovative spirit in career guidance, however, has had little impact on career counseling. Most agency and school counselors continue to apply the vocational counseling procedures initiated by Parsons in 1909 and refined by Williamson (1939, 1949). Few new career counseling procedures are being developed, and in searching for them, one finds that such approaches are not widely publicized or well known.

Counselors, however, need to consider new career counseling

approaches; their innovations in other areas of guidance will create demand for more effective counseling and will free the counselor to do more counseling. Junior college counselors especially need such procedures since the junior college is designed for career development. Consequently, this monograph was commissioned by the Educational Resources Information Center for Junior Colleges to describe and evaluate effective career counseling procedures in a manner that would encourage counselors to try them.

The monograph focuses exclusively on counseling because improvements in other aspects of guidance are already known and operating. The collection of counseling methods presented includes procedures for helping persons to implement plans as well as to make choices. Increasingly, people's careers are involving a series of choices and adaptations, and counselors need to be ready to assist them over the continuum of the career and not merely at the point of choosing a vocation (Morril and Forest, 1970). Most of the procedures are designed for application by a counselor with an individual or small group, but the monograph includes descriptions of self-administering and computer counseling procedures.

The monograph presents only counseling procedures which are replicable in order to help counselors to learn, to improve, and to demonstrate accountability. A procedure is replicable when it can be described in sufficient detail so that counselors can apply it in a uniform manner. Such detailed description facilitates learning. Likewise, by definition, replicable procedures divide into components for accomplishing the steps a client needs for his specific goals and, consequently, they enable the counselor both to show how each counseling session assists his client and to determine which components are working or need improvement (Bergin, 1970; Crites and Brayfield, 1964; Whiteley, 1967). Indeed, it appears that only by adopting replicable procedures can counselors meet the public's growing demand for accountability. Certainly accountability legislation for counselors in states like California indicate that the public expects counselors to improve their services by the kind of systematic study which replicable procedures permit.

Introduction

The replicable procedures presented here were located through an intensive search of the professional literature, a stratified survey of 200 junior college counseling centers, and a conference of 55 counselors from 27 Southern California junior colleges. Thirteen distinct career counseling procedures suitable for adolescents and adults emerged from the search, and they are the major focus of this monograph.

The monograph contains five chapters. In Chapter 1 the concept of replicable counseling is defined to provide a framework for reviewing the thirteen replicable procedures. Chapter 2 presents and reviews procedures which provide assistance in accomplishing the basic vocational developmental tasks suggested by theorists such as Ginzberg (1951, 1972) and Super (1951, 1957, 1963). Chapter 3 describes procedures for resolving special difficulties faced by subpopulations of junior college students such as homemakers, disadvantaged youth, and adults changing occupations. Chapter 4 summarizes the similarities and differences among the procedures and notes their general limitations. Chapter 5 concludes the report by reviewing methods of evaluating career counseling development.

It is beyond the scope of this monograph to present methods for developing proficiency in the thirteen procedures. But others have described training methods, and they should be consulted when building a training program for any of the procedures presented here. For example, recent studies of preservice training by Carkhuff (1969, 1972), Kagen (1969), and Ivey (1971) indicate how counselors can proficiently adopt replicable procedures by practicing specific components and modifying their performance on the basis of feedback from video recordings, peers, and counselor trainers. Community college counselors could use similar techniques by forming inservice groups whose members would role play the components of a procedure, discuss their delivery of each component, and repeat the exercise until their delivery is appropriate. The individual counselor could then try the procedure live, monitor his performance, and adjust it in accord with the principles of formative evaluation (Sorenson, 1971). Counselors can monitor their performance by audio or video recordings of their sessions, by taking notes during or after counseling, by asking clients to recall what happened in their sessions, and by testing client achievement of the component's goal.

Research on preservice counselor training has also shown that modeling facilitates development of competencies (Bandura, 1969; Carkhuff, 1972). Although commercial recordings of the thirteen procedures are not available, Aubrey and Hosford (1971) have suggested that professional counselors work as co-counselor teams or counselor-observer teams to obtain the benefits of modeling. This approach could be adopted for the procedures discussed in this monograph.

ACKNOWLEDGMENTS

M ANY PEOPLE HAVE contributed to the completion of this monograph: the authors of the procedures, the community college counselors who shared their practices and attended the UCLA conference, the UCLA counseling students who assisted in developing the procedure and clarifying the concept of replicability, and the ERIC Junior College Clearinghouse staff. I sincerely appreciate their help. I am especially indebted, however, to my two research assistants, Ann Fogel and Betty Johnson, for their help in gathering data and in reacting to my interpretation of that data. I must also thank Garth Sorenson, for stimulating and assisting me to examine counseling from the perspective of replicability, to Florence Brawer and Arthur Cohen for recognizing the need for this monograph and for their many helpful comments on the presentation of the report, and to my wife, Margaret, for helping me to formulate the ideas of this monograph and for her patience during the months in which this report was being completed.

LIST OF TABLES

Table   I   Classes of Counselor Responses 7
Table   II   Guidelines for Group Counseling at
             Modesto Junior College 43
Table III   Phases of Guided Inquiry Counseling 51
Table   IV   Differences Among 13 Counseling Procedures 67
Table   V   Career Counseling Criteria 76

CONTENTS

	Page
Preface	v
Introduction	vii
Acknowledgments	xi
List of Tables	xiii

Chapter
1. REPLICABLE COUNSELING AND ITS IMPLICATIONS 3
2. COUNSELING PROCEDURES TO AID IN CAREER CHOICE 12
3. COUNSELING PROCEDURES FOR RESOLVING DEFICITS IN
   VOCATIONAL DEVELOPMENT 38
4. OVERVIEW OF THIRTEEN REPLICABLE CAREER
   COUNSELING PROCEDURES 66
5. METHODS OF EVALUATING CAREER DEVELOPMENT 73

Appendices 87
Bibliography 129
Index 135

CAREER COUNSELING IN THE COMMUNITY COLLEGE

CHAPTER 1

REPLICABLE COUNSELING AND ITS IMPLICATIONS

REPLICABLE COUNSELING procedures have been heralded as the means to improve counseling. Yet no published counseling procedure has been termed replicable, and the theorists who have written about the need for replicable procedures have not delineated the characteristics of such a procedure. Since replicability refers to some degree of similarity between two phenomena, its application to counseling processes requires designation of the elements to be repeated; that is, are words, gestures, ideas, atmospheres, etc., to be replicated? The decision cannot be arbitrary if it is remembered that the purpose of a replicable procedure is to improve counseling by permitting differentiation of those components which assist clients from those that do not. For one can then argue that the impact of counseling derives from the information to which the client is exposed and the interaction he experiences, and counselors will wish to replicate ideas and atmospheres. In the following pages replicable counseling is defined, and the characteristics of a replicable procedure are delineated to provide the reader with a model for considering the procedures described in Chapters 2 and 3.

DEFINITION

Counseling is replicable to the extent that persons with comparable goals and obstacles are exposed to the same ideas in equivalent atmospheres. Theoretically, a client's experience would be the same with different counselors. Two persons need not experience counseling in identical ways for it to be replicable since they do not have identical goals or obstacles. Consequently, counseling will never be duplicated. However, insofar as obstacles and goals are comparable, the counselor can acquaint different clients with the same principles in equivalent atmospheres.

In replicable counseling the focus is on what the counselor does. His actions with different clients need not be identical, but the class of his actions and the set of counseling substeps through which he guides both the clients must be the same.[1] For example, if the counselor praises (action) one client every time he says that he will try to solve his problems, he can replicate the procedure with a second client by rewarding (class of action) such statements. With the second client, the counselor need not be restricted to verbal praise nor the same words; he need only insure that his actions are reinforcing. Likewise, in a career counseling procedure with substeps in which a client evaluates himself and different occupations on a set of characteristics, he might first evaluate himeslf and then the different occupations or vice versa. In both instances the counselor guides the client through the same substeps although their sequence differs. Counseling procedures in which the counselor uses the same actions at identical points of the process are standardized as well as replicable. A counseling procedure, however, need not be standardized to be replicable.

Replicable counseling spotlights the role of the counselor during achievement of the client's goal. It emphasizes the undertaking of specific actions to influence the client's behavior. In a real sense he provides a learning program for the client. This recognition that counseling is a type of learning program makes it clear that developing a replicable counseling procedure requires defining: (1) the goals and subgoals, (2) the components, and (3) the indices by which a counselor can regulate the program's occurrence.

GOALS. Counseling is a purposeful relationship for achieving client goals. Task analysis of these goals and appraisal of the

---
[1] In some cases learning substeps have to be sequential because one is based upon the other.

client's skills and experience indicate what has to be learned; that is, what subgoals must be mastered to realize the goal. For example, to process information, one requires an objective and knowledge about appropriate information sources. If one has been unsuccessful in processing information previously, he may also need special support while formulating an objective and while learning about sources of information. A counseling program designed for a specific goal includes components for accomplishing each of the subgoals. Thus, a counseling procedure designed to assist a person who has been a failure in processing information would include components on goal setting, sources of information, and on reconciliation of doubts about success.

COMPONENTS OF COUNSELING. A component of counseling is the combination of exercises (such activities as a test interpretation, discussion of work history, etc.) and counselor responses designed to achieve the program's subgoals. A task analysis of each subgoal indicates the principles, information, or skills that are needed to achieve the subgoal, and the counselor selects or develops exercises for teaching the principles, information, or skills. As the client performs the exercise, the counselor responds in a manner which maximizes the possibility that the exercise works as intended. These responses should not be random but rather should reflect the counselor's beliefs about learning and personality theory. To construct a replicable counseling component, therefore, one must first describe the counseling exercise and then define the set of appropriate counselor responses. But in order to define appropriate responses, one must also categorize client responses and enumerate the rules by which counselor responses relate to client responses. The following paragraphs discuss counselor responses, client responses, and rules for relating them.

Counselor responses are intended to support and complement the exercise of the learning program by influencing client behavior. For example, a counselor who asks a client to discuss his concern (exercise) can elicit a fuller discussion if he reinforces (response) the client as he is discussing his concerns. Counselor responses should encourage the client to act (think, feel, behave, perceive) in a way which has been found to enable the component to work. The specific content of a response is determined by the particular client, but the class of a response is prescribed by the learning program; that is, the learning program says reinforce, but the specific reinforcement depends upon whom the client is. Since counselor responses facilitate the client's use of the learning program; they can be classified in terms of their relation to it in the following manner: (1) explaining the meaning of the program's information; (2) involving the client in the program; (3) diagnosing and evaluating a client's suitability for, and progress in the program; (4) rewarding compliance with the program; (5) advising; and (6) problem solving. Each category is bipolar. The counselor can clarify or confuse; he can involve or ignore his client; he can evaluate or defer judgment, etc. Table I provides a fuller description of each response category.

One method of classifying client reactions is to define their relation to the subgoal of the particular counseling component. By such a method, most client responses can be categorized as follows: (1) complying with the intention of the subgoal; (2) seeking information in order to comply, (3) ignoring or remaining uninvolved in the program; (4) failing to comply with the intention of the subgoal because of lack of skill; and (5) refusing to comply. Refusal is manifested in several ways: declining to follow instructions; questioning the credibility of the counselor; attacking the credibility of the counseling process; or diverting the process to other topics. With a counselor response classification and a client reaction classification, a limited number of rules can specify which counselor responses are appropriate for a specific client action.

The rules of counseling are the counselor's operational definition of learning theory. They reflect his belief about how he can help a person use the learning program's exercises. For example, one counselor might follow the rule of reinforcing compliance with an exercise because he believes that the frequency of an action is increased by reinforcement of it. Another counselor might ask clients to clarify unclear statements. This clarification of their responses can be used to help involve clients in

TABLE I

CLASSES OF COUNSELOR RESPONSES

1. *Explanation of program information* is the class of responses which help clients to understand a principle or procedure of the program. It includes answering questions directly and accurately as well as encouraging questions.
2. *Involving clients* is the class of responses which encourages client participation. To involve clients, a counselor might ask open-ended questions and allow time for responses; redirect one client's question to another client; help a client to realize and examine his similarities to another client; point out how a client's background relates to the current topic; reflect the feeling of a client's communication, wait patiently for the client to talk, and remind clients of their need to participate.
3. *Diagnosis or evaluation* is the class of responses made to the flow of information before and during counseling. If the indices of progress or problems are forthcoming, the counselor need only process information. If the indices do not appear, the counselor asks questions in order to determine the client's progress in accomplishing the subgoals. For example, in helping clients to select occupations for exploration, a counselor first ascertains whether a client has an objective. (When a client is without an objective, the counselor tries various ways of assisting him to specify it, and he attends to the client's responses in order to know when the objective is clarified. He can then proceed in helping him to select occupations for exploration.)
4. *Reinforcement is the class of responses* for increasing the frequency of client compliance with the program's intention. It includes counselor verbal praise, securing group recognition for success, allowing a client to do something he enjoys—e.g. telling his positive feelings about accomplishing a goal, completing only partially correct client statements rather than labeling them as incorrect, etc.
5. *Advising is the class of responses* which informs the client of what the counselor would do. It includes urging, recommending, referring, persuading, etc.
6. *Problem solving is the class of responses* to help a client who cannot proceed in a component. If a person cannot proceed, the counselor can furnish him additional information or assist him in acquiring the skill necessary to proceed. When a client does not proceed, the counselor might guide him to examine the consequences of not continuing, confront him with the inconsistency of his wishes and behavior, urge him to identify and take action against the obstacles to his continuation, ask the client to defer his criticism until he is further along in the process, motivate him by pointing to a fellow client who is succeeding, in group, ignore non-productive client actions by redirecting the focus to a client who is behaving positively.

the counseling, tell clients of the counselor's concern for them, or show clients how to perceive themselves more clearly. Rules can be extracted from the theories of Skinner, Gagne, Ausubel, Rogers, etc.

Since the rules derive from learning theory, it is to be expected that many counselors will use similar ones. Clients are typically reinforced for complying with the intent of the counselor's stimuli, even by client-centered counselors (Truax, 1966); clients who say they are confused usually receive an explanation. Most counselors will attempt to involve clients who are not participating, and they will engage in some form of problem solving when there are obstacles to compliance.

Even when two counselors apply similar rules, the content of their counseling sessions may be different. First, the counseling exercises exert considerable control over the material which the client introduces. For example, a counselor who is an expert in test interpretation will tend to use test interpretation exercises; the client-centered counselor, however, will only infrequently use such an exercise (Patterson, 1964). Secondly, counselors disagree about the appropriate content of the response categories, that is, what is involving or conducive to problem solving. They even disagree about whether all categories are legitimate in counseling. Advising and evaluating are inimical to Rogers (1961), but they are essential to the counseling of Williamson (1939, 1949).

INDICES OF COUNSELING COMPONENTS. In applying a counseling procedure, the counselor must insure that components defining the procedure are accomplishing their objective. For this, he needs to have indices (criteria) against which he can judge the effectiveness of a component and thus know when to proceed to the next component. The counseling program must specify the behaviors which indicate when a component is working. Indices should be client actions or client-counselor interactions because the counseling program is designed to induce learning. Indicators of progress should, thus, be acts which reflect what the client is doing. Indices might include such client actions as asking questions, obtaining information, giving examples, talking more positively about oneself, and completing counseling assignments.

In summary, a counseling procedure will be replicable when a counselor can state the goals and subgoals which a particular population must accomplish, when he can specify counseling components which assist members of that population in accomplishing each subgoal, and when he can identify client behaviors (thoughts, feelings, actions, attitudes) which reflect accomplishment of the subgoals. By defining these as criteria, one insures that the attainment of replicability results in accountability which requires relating the steps by which clients achieve specific goals to specific counselor actions. Likewise, a procedure which meets the criteria or replicability can be improved through systems analysis since, with such a procedure, a counselor can examine how individual counseling components are functioning and, consequently, can know where counseling needs improvement.

In Chapters 2 and 3, the thirteen replicable procedures of this report are described in terms of goals, components, validity, and use on junior college campuses. The counselor responses described in Table I are appropriate for most procedures and, consequently, are not repeated in the component's description of each procedure. The rules for relating counselor responses to client responses and the indices of counseling can readily be inferred from the description of the counseling components. They are not, therefore, included in the description of each procedure.

IMPLICATIONS OF REPLICABILITY

The remainder of this chapter considers the implications of replicability for group counseling, the evolution of career counseling, and the tradition of eclecticism in counseling.

REPLICABILITY AND GROUP COUNSELING. Ideally, a counselor could insure that his client would experience only the ideas and atmosphere needed for achieving his goal. In group counseling such an ideal is not as easily achieved as in individual counseling. The learning program provided by the counselor is modified by the group members. They actually share in the counselor's role since their actions affect the operation of the learning program. Group members model, cue each other, explain or confuse the stimuli of the learning program, involve or distract each other, etc.

Group counseling can nonetheless approach replicability. Client participation can be partially controlled by designing roles for clients, which complement the program, and by informing clients about their roles. For example, peers frequently can help one another by modeling appropriate action, by involving one another in the process, and by rewarding each other for compliance with the program. To activate this group resource, the counselor can tell clients how to learn from each other, and he can model helping behavior and reinforce clients for helping and imitating each other. Well defined client roles can be supplemented by techniques for correcting the misdirection or misinformation that one client gives to another when he digresses from the prescribed client role. These techniques can be included under the problem-solving response category.

Counselors will need additional training to obtain the benefits of replicable group counseling since group work requires greater alertness and a larger repertoire of techniques for guiding clients. Greater investment in counselor training, however, can increase the number of clients served, and it can enable clients to have models and peer support which would not otherwise be available. Psychologists and educators are only beginning to realize the potential of imitative learning and peer motivation. By careful planning, counselors can add these powerful components to their learning programs and still have the potential for systematically evaluating what they are doing.

EVOLUTION OF CAREER COUNSELING. Replicability will change career counseling in the same way that Parsons and Williamson changed it. Both men added system and new technology to the tools of the counselor but left intact the concept that vocational counseling is a process of helping the individual to use his rationality in planning a career. Similarly, replicability will enable counselors to become more systematic in applying the principles of learning when aiding a person to use his rationality in career planning. Indeed, Williamson wrote so clearly about vocational counseling that his system approaches replicability and is described among the potentially replicable procedures.

ECLECTICISM AND REPLICABILITY. Ecelcticism is the practice of using components from several schools of counseling to fashion treatment for the particular needs of one's client. Many counselors pride themselves in being eclectic; the strong tradition of eclecticism in counseling indicates both the openness of counselors to new ideas and their willingness to learn from experience. If an eclectic approach is to improve practice, however, the counselor must be able to specify what he does and what impact his actions have; that is, ecelcticism must involve replicable counseling components. Without replicability the counselor could never be sure what it was that produced different effects with different clients.

In Chapters 2 and 3 of this monograph, thirteen career counseling procedures are described in detail. When reading the detailed descriptions, many counselors will wonder whether combinations of the components from two or more of the procedures would not suit their clients' needs better than either one of the procedures alone or several procedures in tandem. Indeed, it is the counselor's professional responsibility to consider and test such an hypothesis. It is hoped that the presentation of the counseling procedures as sets of components will facilitate trial of new combinations of components. Certainly there is nothing in the procedures which prevents recombining components. Most of the counselor responses listed in Table 1 can be used with all of them. A counselor can be consistent in his responses to his client regardless of whether the components in the counseling program come from one or from several procedures.

The procedures have been described here as distinct from each other only because they have been employed and investigated in that way. But as more research accumulates about the effectiveness of these components, it is conceivable that the unit of description will become the component rather than the procedure. Counselors will then be able to more easily fulfill their responsibility for custom-making procedures for their clientele by choosing from the array of components.

A case in point is made by Bates and Sorenson (1973) who recently suggested a process to be followed in constructing a replicable, custom-made procedure. Their process may be summarized in the following six steps:

1. Identify a goal for a particular population.
2. Specify the subgoals which the members of that population must accomplish in order to achieve the goal.
3. Select or construct counseling components for each subgoal.
4. Identify client behaviors or client-counselor interactions which reflect accomplishment of each subgoal.
5. Try the set of components on a sample of the population to determine which components accomplish the subgoals.
6. Replace components which are not effective, and recycle the set of components with new samples from the population until a set of satisfactory components is achieved.

CHAPTER 2

COUNSELING PROCEDURES TO AID IN CAREER CHOICE

Chapter 2 presents seven career counseling procedures which approach replicability and which are designed to systematically aid clients with several vocational developmental tasks. The procedures include: Williamson's trait-factor vocational counseling, Ryan's reinforcement vocational counseling, Ryan's simulation-reinforcement counseling, Healy's career counseling, case study vocational counseling, Magoon's effective problem solving, and the System of Interaction Guidance and Information (SIGI). Each procedure guides the client through the steps of considering and formulating career goals, recalling or discovering assets, learning about opportunities consistent with his assets and goals, and reviewing and/or applying problem solving and planning principles to his own or a similar client's career concerns.

The rationales behind the seven procedures are similar. Each assumes that systematic consideration of the elements of planning will increase knowledge about planning and planning activities, and persons are more likely to be satisfied and successful in occupations which are compatible with their talents, interests, temperament and values. The Ryan and Healy procedures explicitly incorporate provision for cueing and reinforcing planning; the Williamson, Ryan, case study, and EPS procedures explicitly incorporate use of vocational testing; and the Healy and case study procedures directly encourage and provide the opportunity for clients to help one another in planning. Although explicit in only some procedures, systematic reinforcement, utilization of vocational testing results and peer assistance are compatible with all procedures. Utilization of such methods is widely supported in the counseling literature (Krumboltz, 1969; Osipow and Walsh, 1970; Super, 1949; Tyler, 1969). Williamson alone assumes that the counselor is best able to organize and draw conclusions from client data, but this assumption is not supported by empirical data (Hewer, 1966; Kelly and Fiske, 1951).

Four of the procedures have been designed for group counseling—Ryan's two procedures, Healy's procedure, and case study counseling. The Williamson procedure could also be adapted for groups. In the Magoon procedure, a client completes a series of paper-pencil exercises and receives written feedback concerning his performance from a counselor. In SIGI, the client interacts with a computer by exploring the feasibility of satisfying his values within different occupations. Neither of the latter provides for interaction in a group.

The first five procedures are described from the perspective of the model for replicable counseling presented in Chapter 1. The effective Problem Solving Approach has been described in detail in Krumboltz and Thoresen (1969), and so it will only be summarized here. Since SIGI is a computer program, not amenable to the same type of description as the other procedures, only a summary description of it is presented.

WILLIAMSON'S PROCEDURE

Trait factor counseling evolved from the work of Parsons (1909) and from advances in psychological testing into the most widely used approach in vocational counseling. It has had several prominent advocates, but unquestionably Williamson (1939, 1949) has been the foremost among them. Thus the description of the procedure which is presented here relies heavily on Williamson.

The objective of Williamson's or trait factor vocational counseling is to get the client to try out an educational program and an occupational choice which has potential for success and satisfaction. When approaching the objective, each client receives a thorough survey of personal and environmental factors relevant to choosing and entering an occupation, an explanation of how his personal traits relate to occupational opportunities, and a review of possible courses of action. Each client participates in the survey, development of an explanation, and a review of possible courses of action to the extent of his ability and interest. Today, counselors using the trait factor approach stress the need for the client's active involvement and understanding of all phases of the counseling process. The six phases are inception, reconnaissance, hypothesis development, hypothesis dissemination, planning, and the follow-up phase. Williamson termed the phases, "analysis, synthesis, diagnosis, prognosis, counseling, and follow up." The following section details the exercises and the responses which Williamson used to create the atmosphere and to generate the information and ideas needed for making vocational choices.

METHOD. In the inception phase, the counselor greets the client, invites him to be comfortable, and initiates discussion about the client's vocational indecision. The counselor himself is calm, attentive, and deliberate; this sets the stage for planning. (Today, this would be termed modeling.) He proceeds to elicit the client's expectations about counseling, and he helps the client to correct any misunderstandings about the process. He insures that the client realizes that choosing an occupation is a "logical process of collecting, reviewing, evaluating, accepting and rejecting the evidence of experience, school, grades, psychological tests, and other data." Inception is successful when the client indicates that he understands the processes of counseling and choosing an occupation.

The reconnaissance is next.[1] The objective of this phase is to collect data relevant to the client's decision. The counselor decides what information to gather and when to stop gathering it. Before counseling and between sessions, he reviews anecdotal records, autobiographies, questionnaires, psychological tests, and inventories to begin developing a picture of the client. His review of materials in light of his clinical experience and the client's

---

[1] The term reconnaissance was chosen because this aspect of Williamson's counseling is very similar to the reconnaissance explicated in detail by H. A. Sullivan in the *Psychiatric Interview*, 1953.

expressed concerns suggest the probing which he does during the interview and any psychological tests he may prescribe. Williamson has recommended gathering a broad range of data, including information about abilities, achievements, family background, response to counseling, time usage, health, recreational pursuits, hobbies, work experiences, interests, and expectations of significant others. Open-ended questions, reflection of feeling, parapharasing, and expectant silence are especially useful in this type of probing.

As information accumulates, the counselor develops hypotheses about its meaning for the client's vocational choice. He weighs each datum in terms of its representativeness and tells the client his reason for differential weighing of data. Tests and inventories are regarded highly because of their reliability, but Williamson urges obtaining data about a characteristic from multiple sources. From the accumulated data, the counselor "teases out" hypotheses and encourages the client to join him. However, he presents the client with only those data which he judges relevant. To evaluate progress, the client can be asked to describe the information and hypotheses which have been developed.

Williamson believes that each counselor must develop his own hypothesis building and prognostic procedure. He describes the process of developing hypotheses generally, rather than specifically. It is not, consequently, replicable. He urges the counselor to verify his hypothetical picture against the client's reactions during planning and his efforts at implementation during follow-up. This is to improve the counselor's hypothesis building capacity. Williamson suggests that the counselor ponder a broad spectrum of questions when creating a picture of the client, insisting that the counselor consider aptitude before interest in weighing the feasibility of choices. The hypothesis development phase continues even as counseling moves into the hypothesis dissemination and planning phases.

In the dissemination phase, the counselor presents his hypotheses in non-technical language. He attends closely to the client's reaction, using that feedback to decide whether and how to clarify his explanation. He does not use charts or other aids for fear he will be unable to observe the client. He verifies that the client understands his explanation because he is relying on its logic to induce the client to act. If he is confident about his hypothesis, he presents it persuasively. If there are competing alternatives, he gives the evidence for each. The organization of data has been determined by the counselor's picture of the person and thus, has not been replicated. However, a standardized format for disseminating information would enable this aspect of trait factor counseling to approach replicability.

After the client understands the counselor's appraisal, client and counselor consider implications for various choices: major, occupation, or transfer. Options introduced by the client are considered first. (To accomplish planning, the counselor is expected to be acquainted with the range of options open to his clients). The counselor indicates how the data support, or oppose, different courses of action. He ranks plans in terms of feasibility and indicates how one would be chosen. He advises rather than "dictates." Williamson offers the following example of this type of presentation:

> As far as I can tell from this evidence of aptitude, your chances of getting into the medical school are poor; but your possibilities in business seem to be much more promising. These are the reasons for my conclusions: You have done consistently failing work in zoology and chemistry. You do not have the pattern of interests characteristic of successful doctors which probably indicates you would not find the practice of medicine congenial. On the other hand, you do have an excellent grasp of mathematics, good general ability, and the interests of an accountant. These facts seem to me to argue for your selection of accountancy as an occupation. Suppose you think about these facts and my suggestion, talk to your father about my suggestion, see Professor Blank who teaches accounting, and return next Tuesday at 10 o'clock to tell me what conclusion you have reached. I urge that you weigh the evidence pro and con for your choice. (Williamson, 1949)

Counseling does not conclude until the counselor follow-up has determined the outcome. Follow-up benefits both client and counselor. It shows the client that the counselor is concerned and enables him to renew counseling if necessary. It permits the counselor to verify the accuracy of his hypotheses. Indeed, this step is essential if the counselor is to develop the clinical sense necessary to generate the useful hypotheses for which the procedures makes him responsible.

VALIDITY AND USE IN JUNIOR COLLEGE. In most reports of vocational counseling research, the counseling procedure has not been defined. Consequently, even though Williamson's procedure has been used extensively, definitive research about it is not available. Certainly, it can be assumed that much of the vocational counseling of demonstrated worth has been patterned after Williamson; his has been the major method of *vocational* counseling since the 1930s (Samler, 1962; Tyler, 1969).

When asked about the sequence followed in career counseling junior college counselors indicated that they used the Williamson sequence more than any other. Robert Meshanic, of Suffolk County Community College, New York, describes the sequence: "Initial interview and determination of testing—arrival at decisions in terms of occupational and career choices—selection of sequences of courses." At Cabrillo College, California prospective clients are given a ten-step plan, detailing the Williamson procedure, to inform them about vocational counseling (Appendix A).

REPLICABILITY The inception and information dissemination phases of Williamson's procedure are well described and do approach replicability. His data gathering techniques are also presented clearly and could be partially replicated by administering a battery of tests, inventories, and a biographical questionnaire. The clinical interviewing aspect of data gathering, however, needs to be defined more precisely in order to be replicable. A counselor interested in defining a replicable interview should consult Williamson's *Student Counseling* (1939), *Counseling Adolescents* (1949), and H. S. Sullivan's *Psychiatric Interview* (1953) for specific ideas about the manner and extent of probing needed.

On the other hand, Williamson's methods for developing hypotheses and prognoses about different plans are not sufficiently detailed to be replicable. He maintains that hypothesis generation is the essence of the art of counseling; this cannot be replicated.

However, as computer technology develops, it is becoming possible to define and thus, to replicate the steps of hypothesis generation and selection. Computers now provide clinical interpretations of the *Strong Vocational Interest* and the *Minnesota Multiphasic Personality Inventory* (Fowler, 1968). Soon a computer will be able to analyze a counselor's hypothesis development and program that process. Then the counselor need only provide appropriate data for the computer to generate hypotheses in a replicable manner.

Even today, however, the counselor who wishes to rely on tests and inventories can have the benefits of computer technology in hypothesis generation and selection. The College Entrance Examination Board and the American Council of Testing (ACT) have developed similar testing programs which provide hypotheses about the relative merits of different occupational training programs for a high school graduate/young adult. The ACT program, entitled the Career Planning Program (CPP), includes assessing a student's interests, values, abilities, and accomplishments; the data, analyzed by computer, furnishes both prognostic indications of success potential for training in different vocational-technical programs and indications of student similarities in such programs. The prognostic statements are similar to explanations generated by Williamson, but they are based upon regression equations and discriminant analysis, instead of counselor judgment. The CPP data are also presented in a well organized, understandable manner. Even though a procedure combining the CPP with Williamson's inception and dissemination phases of counseling ignores some clinical aspects, it would still be classified as a replicable trait factor procedure.

RYAN'S PROCEDURES

At Blue Mountain Community College (Pendleton, Oregon), Ryan (1968) has developed and tested two group career counseling procedures. The objectives are for a client to learn and apply career decision making skills. In the first procedure, designated here as the reinforcement method, the client's secondary objectives are that he: (1) consider his aspirations and characteristics,

(2) consider and use methods for learning about occupations and training programs, (3) set immediate occupational training goals, and (4) ponder future possibilities. In the second procedure, described here as the simulation-reinforcement method, clients as a group accomplish the subgoals of producing immediate and future plans for students, like themselves but fictitious. Both methods were designed to complement a vocational guidance class, which included vocational testing and its interpretation, as well as lectures about the world of work.

The general atmosphere to be created in the two procedures is similar. Consequently, the means for achieving it are described here for both procedures. The procedures differ in the substep phase of achieving counseling goals; the substeps are, therefore, described for each procedure. Following the description of the procedures, data pertinent to their validity are reviewed.

METHOD. Each procedure requires ten fifty-minute sessions in addition to twenty hours of class. Forty minutes of each session are devoted to content, and the remaining time is used for opening and closing the sessions. During the main part of the session, the counselor is responsible for providing requested information, giving verbal cues in order to elicit responses related to decision making, and reinforcing decision-making responses. Verbal cues include such leading questions as, "Where do you think_____(name)_____ might find information about job openings in this area?" Throughout the session the counselor is warm and attentive, and he encourages the group members to act in the same way. In the two to five minute opening, he greets the clients and establishes rapport. At the first meeting, the counselor asks the clients to introduce themselves. He then describes the activities which are planned for the ten sessions. In the two to five minute closing, he interrupts counseling by saying something like, "Ok, I see the time is up for today. I am looking forward to seeing you next week. We had a good session. Some of the things which we discussed today will be helpful to you in planning, and I hope that you will think about them." In other words, he ends on a positive note while setting the stage for subsequent meetings.

REINFORCEMENT PROCEDURE. In this procedure, the counselor

guides his group through ten topics by asking a series of cue questions pertinent to specific points. The topics and the cue questions are presented below, and Appendix B presents a sample dialogue from the reinforcement procedure.

1. Looking at the present: Orientation session.
    What kind of person are you?
    What kind of person do you want to be?
    Why did you come to a community college?
    What do you think of yourself at this time?
    What problems do you have?
    What are your long term goals?
    How do you decide on goals (Personal factors/ occupational information)?
2. Looking at yourself: Personal factors to consider in choosing a vocation.
    How do personal interests influence choice?
    How do personality characteristics influence choice?
    What about intelligence?
    What about health, physical characteristics?
    What about special aptitudes?
3. Looking at the world of work: Occupational information to consider in choosing a vocation or looking at occupations (general orientation to importance of occupational information).
    What vocational-technical opportunities are likely in this area?
    What are requirements for career entry in different jobs?
    What are chances of getting work in various jobs?
    What training or education is required for different jobs?
    What are the rewards: advancement, financial, security, transfer possibility, personal satisfaction?
4. Finding out about oneself: Sources of information.
    Where to find out about yourself?
    Test data: What do they mean?
    School records: What do they suggest?
    Self-evaluation: What do you think of yourself?
    Professional evaluation: What do others think?

5. Finding out about the world of work and leisure: Sources of information.
   Where to find out about the world of work and leisure?
      Library references.
      Local resources.
      Occupational files.
      Employment office.
6. Considering occupational areas: Deliberating about alternatives.
   How to relate personal information and occupational information.
   How to consider consequences of different alternatives.
7. Considering educational and training programs for possible vocational choices.
   Looking at personal characteristics.
      What learning problems do you have?
      What special aptitudes, personality characteristics, and interests do you have?
   Looking at educational and training programs.
      What are entrance requirements?
      What is the cost?
      What is availability of program?
8. Deciding on an immediate vocational goal.
   What is your choice of an occupational goal?
      Why did you select this occupation?
9. Deciding on an educational or training program to reach the vocational goal.
   What kind of preparation do you need?
   Where can you get the training?
10. Looking into the future.
    What kind of person are you?
    What kind of person do you want to be?
    Do you belong in a big organization or a small one?
    Do you belong in a pressure-job?
    Do you belong in a job demanding careful, detailed work?
    Do you want to take risks and chances?
    How can you keep your career options open?

What are your long term goals?
How will you make decisions about work throughout your life?
How can you find out about the need for making decisions to change you: life plan?

Ryan did not indicate the principles to be discovered from each cue question, although principles were discussed during the training of counselors. For example, from the cue question about the influence of interests on choice, one might discover that different occupations use different interests and that persons in the same occupation have similar interests. Specification of principles is essential to enable a counselor to know when to proceed to the next cue question. Although many counselors will agree about most of the principles to be elicited, disagreements may occur unless the principles are specified. To make the procedure replicable, therefore, the reader/counselor should designate the essential principles to be discovered by the clients from each cue question.

SIMULATION METHOD. In the second of the Ryan methods, the simulation-reinforcement procedure, the counselor guides his group in designing plans for five fictitious students deemed similar to Blue Mountain students. In introducing each case, the counselor tells the group: "You will be helping to plan the life of an individual for the four years after high school. You will get to know him, his likes and dislikes, his background, and his abilities. As you plan his life, you will begin to consider alternatives which occur each time a decision is made. You will discuss the consequences of his decision" (Ryan, 1968).

At the opening of each session, the counselor reminds the clients that their purpose is to develop planning skills. He informs them that they may ask for information about the consequences of different courses of action for the fictitious student, and he then distributes a case study and points out its essential elements.

A sample student profile is presented in Appendix C. For each case study of this type, the counselor uses cue questions to guide clients examining such aspects of the fictitious student's situation as the following: (Ryan does not specify the aspects to examine, but they are suggested by the transcript of the illustrative counseling session in her report and have been added in order to increase replicability).

1. The kind of person he is—his goals and problems.
2. Personal factors important in career choice—interests, aptitudes, experiences, physical characteristics.
3. Occupational characteristics important in career choice—location, travel requirements, on-going training.
4. Occupational alternatives—the ability of alternatives to meet his needs and utilize his talents.
5. Educational and vocational programs available—their relation to his past experience, their requirements and cost, and their potential for meeting the client's goals.
6. The impact on the client of his choice—the expected life style, the job demands, and the probable rewards.

While the group is discussing the fictitious client's case, the counselor introduces into the scenario such unplanned events as loss of a part-time job or the divorce of parents. These events are designed to provide practice in dealing with chance problems.

VALIDITY AND USE IN JUNIOR COLLEGES. Ryan studied the effects of her procedures with a group of 300 students at Blue Mountain Community College who had scholastic aptitude scores on SCAT or ACT below the 50 percentile or whose vocational goals appeared unrealistic in terms of measured abilities and interests. She compared her treatments with one another, with a nonreinforcement group, and with an inactive control group. Her findings indicate that the reinforcement and simulation procedures increased deliberation about decision making and knowledge about sources of occupational information more than the non-reinforcement procedures. The simulation-reinforcement procedure increased deliberation about decisions more than the reinforcement procedure. Using an approach similar to the Ryan reinforcement procedure, Anderson (1970) increased the information seeking of fifty-four counseled veterans and also distinguished between the effects of cues and reinforcement. The combination of cues and reinforcements was found to be most effective in increasing information seeking of the Vietnam veterans in a special program at UCLA designed to assist students with poor academic backgrounds in entering college. Cues without reinforcement evoked information seeking, but reinforcement without cues did not.

THE HEALY PROCEDURE

Healy and his students developed a counseling procedure with the objectives that each client learn career planning and problem-solving skills and apply those skills during the forming of career plans. In achieving these goals, each client identifies his goals and assets, considers the fit of different occupations with his goals and assets, recalls and uses methods of learning about occupations and himself, selects a tentative occupational direction, identifies entryways to occupations of interest to him, and considers strategies for overcoming obstacles to his plans or the plans of people like him.

METHOD. This procedure, which has been used with groups of three to seven clients and with individuals, consists of five sessions, each of which has specific objectives. Although individuals have completed the procedure in five 50 minute sessions, the typical sessoin is 100 minutes long.

The objectives of the first session are to develop a group which will encourage its members to explore their career potential and make plans, give the members an overview of the counseling activities and goals, and allow each client to select at least ten to fifteen work-relevant qualities. To accomplish the first objective, the counselor tells the group that he expects help and learning between members. This means that they must have an understanding of each other. The group members introduce themselves in a manner designed to encourage talk and aquaintanceship with other member's concerns. Each identifies his own concerns and then identifies by name and concern every client who preceded him. The counselor encourages clarifying crosstalk on similarities and differences among group members, and he reminds them that such help is expected.

To accomplish the second objective of this initial session, the counselor describes the counseling procedure and asks different clients to comment on its relevance to their concerns. Questions about the procedure are welcomed. Next, the counselor guides the clients in the selection of work-relevant qualities. These qualities include both the attributes which a client can, or will be able to, bring to a job to perform it, and the benefits he hopes to acquire from working. In introducing the task of choosing work related qualities, the counselor gives examples of traits that can be brought to a job and those that can be acquired from working. In order to insure that the task is understood, clients are asked for examples of qualities. Clients first generate their own list of traits, and then receive a list of qualities to insure that a wide range is considered (Appendix D).

Clients who are unsure about what they will be able to do or what they want to obtain from working are encouraged to generate such principles for proceeding as "skills developed in a school major and in previous jobs will help one in his occupation" and "at work it is pleasant to do what you have enjoyed doing previously."

After every client has a list of qualities, the counselor explains that those a person considers important can give some insight into the person. Clients are asked to share with the group the four or five qualities which are personally most important and then discuss the implications of these qualities for different work roles.

The objectives for session two are that each client understand that a wide range of occupations can be examined by looking closely at a selected few. They examine six such occupations in terms of the qualities selected during the first session, recall different sources of occupational information, and experience, at least vicariously, use of different sources of occupational information.

At the start of session two, in order to spur involvement, a volunteer identifies the other clients and their concerns. Everyone is encouraged to participate. Next, the clients report their experiences with the tasks which they had chosen for themselves in session one, and they recall the first session and their understanding of the total procedure. The counselor then explains the significance of session two in counseling.

To accomplish the first objective, the counselor explains how occupations can be grouped in several ways and helps the clients to recall ways, such as nature of work and level of skill. He notes that if the occupations are grouped and a representative occupation from each group is examined, a wide range of occupations can be surveyed by examining only a few. He elicits discussion so that he can evaluate the clients' comprehension.

Objective two is accomplished when each client rates his concept of the typical person in at least six occupations on the qualities chosen in session one. The counselor asks the clients to list occupations which they might consider entering. He then distributes a sheet with ninety-two occupations grouped into Holland's (1959) six clusters (Appendix E) and helps the clients to discover the basis of each cluster. Each client proceeds by identifying the clusters to which the occupations he listed belong. Clients with more than one occupation from a cluster are asked to rate only one or two occupations from that cluster. Next, the counselor explains the use of a seven-point rating scale and then illustrates its use by leading the group in rating two or more occupations on some of the qualities which individual members have chosen. Following this, the clients rate each of the occupations they had chosen on their work-relevant traits.

Objective three is met by guiding group members into asking each other for help, analyzing their experience in order to make a specific rating, and noting information which they lack but can plan to obtain. When the group disagrees about a rating or finds it lacks information, the counselor encourages them to recall ways of securing occupational information, such as reading, observing workers, or asking trainers. After the occupational ratings are finished, the counselor asks for reactions and feelings about the ratings. When someone lacks information of interest, the counselor elicits a committment for obtaining the information and sharing the experiences in gathering it at session three.

The objectives of the third session are that each client rate himself accurately on the qualities chosen in session one, recall and use methods of appraisal, and compute the differences between the self and occupational ratings. The clients first report their extracounseling tasks and summarize sessions one and two.

Counseling Procedures to Aid in Career Choice 27

The counselor then explains the need for self-rating and elicits the clients' reactions. About this time, clients usually question the subjectivity of self-ratings and sometimes the subjectivity of the whole procedure. If the clients do not raise the issue of subjectivity, the counselor does. During this discussion, the counselor emphasizes that the procedure depends upon every client's having and reporting ideas about occupations and himself which are realistic and not inflated by social desirability. The clients are helped to recognize that it is in their interest to expend the effort to obtain such knowledge and to recall ways of knowing themselves. For example, clients enumerate ways such as: reviewing and deliberating about one's experiences, taking and receiving interpretations of tests, etc. After rating themselves on the work-relevant qualities, the clients share their reactions, especially concerning those qualities about which they would like more knowledge, and are helped to decide upon methods for obtaining such knowledge.

To accomplish objective three, each client computes the sum of absolute differences between the self and each occupational rating and subtracts that sum from 100 (100-Σ/self-rating-occupation rating/). The self-rating is aligned with each occupational rating, and the differences are added. After inspecting his difference scores in order to determine his similarity to each occupation, the client shares his initial reactions, and the group briefly discusses them.

The objectives of session four are that each client examine the implications of his difference scores in the group and formulate a plan of action consistent with his difference scores. After the report of between-session tasks and a client summary of preceding sessions, clients share their difference scores and their reactions to them. The client who is satisfied with his difference scores examines the implications of entering an occupation, like those in the Holland cluster, to which he is similar. The group members discuss the steps of entering the specific occupation, clarify the need for additional information, and share their reactions to the client's identification with that occupation.

During the interaction, the counselor relates the plans of at least one client to formal planning by labeling the components of his plan. (The planning labels are: set goals, specify and weigh alternatives, select one alternative, carry out plan, and evaluate it.) If the labels of the planning paradigm indicate that the client's plan is incomplete, the group helps him to complete his plan. Subsequent clients are encouraged to use the labels in formulating their plans.

Clients who are dissatisfied with their difference scores are helped to identify the source of their dissatisfaction and to plan corrective action. Those who dislike their identification with specific occupational goups, but feel that such similarity is real, are helped to consider methods by which to change themselves or to examine the implications of accepting the similarity. Those whose difference scores are not differentiated are encouraged to consider the accuracy of their self and occupational ratings. One major reason for lack of differentiation is hasty rating. Thus, they either re-rate the self and the occupations, or they re-examine the sources of difference to determine those qualities in which there are differences among occupations.

The objectives of session five are that the clients report their efforts in implementing their plans and consider problem-solving strategies for overcoming obstacles to their plans. Clients first report their extracounseling tasks and summarize the previous sessions. The clients who rerated and recomputed their difference scores share the results and reactions. The group then considers the implications of entrance into occupations suggested by the new difference scores.

Clients who had made plans in session five discuss their first efforts in implementing those plans. In sharing their experiences, clients are encouraged to specify the concrete actions which can be taken and to reinforce each other in such actions. As plans become more concrete, the counselor asks the group to identify obstacles which might prevent individual clients from executing their plans. The individual client and group then discuss methods for coping with such obstacles. The counselor relates the methods of coping to the steps of problem solving by labeling the components of the solutions and by encouraging the clients to use the labels when discussing the obstacles and the solutions of another client's plans. (The problem solving components are: specify goals, define obstacles, determine alternative solutions, weigh alternatives, select and try alternatives, and evaluate outcome.) The counselor concludes by summarizing the five sessions and by congratulating the clients on their completion of the procedure.

Excerpts from counseling are presented in Appendix F to illustrate those counseling components about which counseling trainees requested clarification. In addition, Appendix F contains the outline of the procedure which is used in rating adherence to it.

VALIDITY AND USE IN JUNIOR COLLEGE. The Healy procedure is derived from Super's (1969) hypothesis: Those occupational choices that are the implementation of the self concept will be more satisfying and productive than those not so related. It asserts that increasing a person's differentiation among occupations in terms of goals and assets helps to make occupational choices. Like the other procedures in this chapter, it assumes that systematic exposure to planning increases the likelihood of successful planning. In implementation, the procedure assumes that the clients are, or can readily become, aware of their goals and assets and the relative ability of different occupational groups to meet those goals and utilize assets.

Data supporting Super's self-concept theory of vocational choice indirectly support the validity of the procedure. Especially noteworthy among those data are findings that professionals perceive that they are in, or are entering, occupations which they feel fit them better than other occupations (Healy, 1968; Hunt, 1967); persons staying in an occupation report and perceive themselves as more like the typical person in that occupation (Strong, 1955); and teachers becoming counselors perceive themselves as more like counselors than teachers (Bingham, 1966; Shiner, 1963).

Two direct studies of the procedure have been made at Santa Monica College in California. In the first study with a group of thirty-five students, twenty-two of the twenty-five who returned follow-up questionnaires felt that they had benefited, and the 25 subjects' mean certainty about their work goals and choices of occupation and major increased significantly after counseling. The counselors felt that twenty-seven of the thirty-five clients progressed; five regressed or made no progress, and three dropped out. Benefits reported by clients included motivation to obtain information and to choose and enter a major (Healy, 1973b).

In the second study a delayed control design was used. Three groups of students started three weeks before the other three groups. Students starting at different times did not differ in certainty about major or occupational goals. After the first groups finished counesling, however, their certainty was significantly higher than those just starting. In addition, mean pre and post indicators of certainty about occupational choice, major, and goals were significantly higher for the twenty-six of thirty-four clients who completed counseling.

The procedure has also been used with one group of junior college women only and with two groups of six bright 12th graders from disadvantaged backgrounds (Washington High School, Los Angeles) who planned to enter college. In the women only group, the counselor felt that much more attention was given to formulating goals appropriate for women than had occurred in the mixed sex groups. During planning, feminine concerns (such as expected size of family, resentment of moving to accommodate a husband's career, etc.) were raised which would not have been raised in a mixed group. The disadvantaged youths completed elements of the first four sessions of the procedure in four one-hour sessions. This required their voluntarily staying one hour after school each week. Analysis of the tapes and their reports indicated that they were involved and found the exercises stimulating.

VOCATIONAL CHOICE CASE STUDY COUNSELING

Counselors at the University of Minnesota and California State University at Hayward adapted the case study for helping clients to either make an occupational choice or to develop a plan for making a choice by analyzing appraisal data about themselves and fellow clients in the context of case studies. Each client presents data from testing and other sources relative to his interests, aptitudes, achievement, and values. He and his group examine the data as if they were staffing a case. As a member of the counseling group, each client organizes his own material in terms of its relevance to occupational choice, and he uses problem-solving techniques and observes others using such techniques in resolving vocational problems.

Hewer and Volsky (1959), at the University of Minnesota, and Sprague and Strong (1971), at California State College at Hayward, successfully employed the case study procedure with college underclassmen. Their procedures are comprised of the following steps: orientation, completion of a battery of tests, interpretation of test results and explanation of other data to be discussed in the case studies, presentation by each client of his appraisal data in a case study format, and periodic progress reports by clients. The exercises and counselor responses of case study counseling are described below along with this author's suggestion for making the procedure replicable.

METHOD. To be replicable, the case study counseling procedure requires that an initial orientation cover the same content each time, that the same tests and inventories be employed and interpreted in the same manner, and that each client focus on specific aspects of his case in his presentation and in his progress report. Clients can focus on specific aspects of a case if standardized questions are asked of the appraisal data and follow-up reports. In the following paragraphs, the three requirements are discussed more fully.

The first session is used to give a detailed explanation of both the counseling process and vocational problem solving, and it provides an opportunity for clients to introduce themselves and their vocational concerns. For replicability, the goals and content of the first group session should be specific. A counselor following this procedure needs to define what his clients have to know about the process itself, about each other, about problem-solving techniques, and about their role in it. For example, the counselor must decide whether they should be able to state the names, the perceived problems, the feelings about the problems, the history of the problem for the other clients, or whether they need to know only that the other clients are concerned about occupational choice.

Several different inventories and tests, including the Strong

Vocational Interest Blank (SVIB), the Kuder Occupational Interest Survey (1966), the General Aptitude Test Battery (1958), the Act Career Planning Program (1972), are appropriate for use in case study counseling as long as the counselor designates the level of interpretation. For example, one might interpret an 'A' on a SVIB scale as indicating an occupation which is more likely to be interesting to the person than one in which he has a 'B' or 'C' score. One might also be more specific and say that few persons enter and stay in occupations in which they have 'C's, but they tend to enter 'A' occupations and are more likely to stay in them (Campbell, 1971). Since age and range of experience influence the reliability of appraisal instruments, each counselor should judge the appropriate level of interpretation for his clients.[2]

The manner in which a client is helped to consider his appraisal data will be replicable if the counselor guides the group in considering a set of standardized questions. For example, when reacting to data from the SVIB, the group could be asked such questions as: What kinds of people are in occupations for which the presenter has primary or secondary interest patterns? Or, if he has no primary or secondary interest patterns, what kinds of people are in occupations in which he has 'A's' and in what kinds of activities do they engage? How do these activities compare to those of the presenter? How could the presenter obtain more information about the occupation?

Next, the group could consider questions such as: What abilities and training are required of persons in occupations of interest to the presenter? How does the presenter's achievements and plans compare with those requirements? What specific courses and experiences are needed to enter such occupations? What additional thinking and planning does he need to do? Finally, each presenter could publicly consider the ways in which his friends and family would react to his membership in the

---

[2] Sprague and Strong (1970) provided clients with written guides to interpreting scores to supplement the group session and Professor Zytowski of the University of Iowa has developed tape-recorded interpretations of the SVIB and Kuder. Such materials can further replicability.

occupation of interest, how his training and occupational duties would influence his lifestyle, and what he would be like five years after entry into the occupation. Although not essential to replicability, a uniform method of reporting one's case would facilitate asking the standardized questions.

VALIDITY. Limited evidence on the effectiveness of the vocational choice case study method is available. Sprague and Strong (1970) reported that twenty-five of thirty-five clients answering follow-up questionnaires responded favorably to participating in such counseling, and Hewer, in a personal communcation, has indicated that students responded favorably to this type of counseling procedure while it was in operation at the University of Minnesota. Applications of the case study to other career problems have not been reported, but inspection of the procedure suggests that it might be adopted for counseling homogeneous groups with career problems, i.e. obtaining employment, relating to a supervisor, etc. Thus, although research is still limited on the effectiveness of case study counseling, it has promise of being a versatile counselor tool.

EFFECTIVE PROBLEM SOLVING

The Effective Problem Solving (EPS) procedure is a series of paper-pencil exercises constructed by Magoon (1969) to help University of Maryland students make occupational choices. It provides clients with an intensive six to eight hour experience in systematically choosing a major and an occupation. Magoon described the procedure fully in Krumboltz and Thoresen (1969) and, consequently, the counseling exercises and counselor responses are only summarized here. Following the summary, studies pertinent to the validity of EPS are reviewed, and suggestions are made concerning the guarantee of replicability.

Method. A series of written exercises guides the client through the steps of defining the problem of occupational choice, obtaining relevant information, weighing the evidence gathered, and choosing among alternative plans or goals. The client answers standardized, open-ended questions about occupational preferences, study skills, time usage, achievement, ability, work experiences, leisure time activities, inventoried interests, and the opinions of others about him. The counselor reviews the answers to each set of questions and points out omissions, inconsistencies, etc. The client proceeds at his own pace, usually taking six to eight one-hour sessions.

While completing initial parts of the inventory, the client lists occupations that he wishes to explore further. He then obtains information and answers the following questions about the occupations: What kind of work is done? What does the work mainly involve—things, data, people? What does the occupation require—education, skills, attitude or interests, other? What are your main strengths for this occupation? Your main weaknesses? How suitable would the job be for you? How suitable would the required education be for you?

The client next utilizes a special form to organize the self and occupational information in one place. This facilitates an occupational choice. Upon reviewing the chart, he chooses three occupational alternatives, describes the actions necessary to enter each, and indicates how dropping out of college would effect pursuit of each of the three occupations.

At specific points in the process, the counselor reviews the client's written work, notes inconsistencies, and makes suggestions, usually in writing, to enable the client to follow EPS. The counselor answers questions, directs the client to questions he has not considered, evaluates the realism and the completeness of the client's knowledge and plans, and encourages him to continue by praising him for persisting; he also helps the client by recalling the benefits of completing EPS. Magoon lists various problems which arise at specific points in the process, and, by implication, he expects a counselor to help his clients resolve such problems. Many of the problems consist of superficial reading of exercises, regarding habits as unchangeable, concern with trivial differences in test scores, frustration and fatigue with difficult parts of the program, etc.

VALIDITY AND USE IN JUNIOR COLLEGE. Entering University of Maryland students who had lower than average academic records have used EPS for several years. These students were generally favorable to completing EPS and indicated that the EPS was as effective or more effective than other counseling they had experienced. Of ninety-two students completing EPS in the period 1966-1968, only 1 percent felt it was of no help; 28 percent reported it to be very helpful; 51 percent thought it quite helpful and 20 percent of some help. Half of these students had had previous counseling, and of these forty-six, 98 percent felt that EPS was more helpful than other counseling.

Graff, Danish, and Austin (1972) contrasted completion of an adaptation of the EPS with traditional, non-replicable individual and group counseling. Their adaptation (Danish, Graff, Gensler, 1969) was significantly more effective than individual or group counseling when helping clients (208 Southern Illinois University students) learn about educational and occupational opportunities, make decisions, and set educational and vocational goals consistent with measured abilities, interests, and personality characteristics. Their self instruction booklet was as effective as individual or group counseling in assisting students to discuss the personal-social factors which affect choice, to relate values to vocational choice, and to interpret and evaluate interest and aptitude tests.

REPLICABILITY. EPS will be replicable if two aspects are clarified. First, when using EPS, the counselor must review the client's progress at several points to insure that the client is considering a sufficient number of realistic alternatives. For example, if a client decided that he was suited for the training and eventual practice of engineering in spite of his low achievement and aptitude for mathematics and science, the counselor would ask him about the discrepancy. The objectives, to be replicable, must be reviewed at each comment point and should be specified so that different counselors could provide uniform feedback. Secondly, the counselor also interprets vocational tests and inventories. For replicability, the rules for test interpretation must be specified in the same manner that the rules for interpretation should be specified in case study counseling.

THE SYSTEM OF INTERACTION, GUIDANCE AND INFORMATION (SIGI)

SIGI was developed by Katz (1969) to assist junior college students to determine which occupations are compatible with their values. There are four components in the program: values, information, prediction, and planning. In the values component, the student learns how career decisions involve choices among competing values, and he is helped to order his own values in terms of their personal importance. In the information component, the student locates occupations which meet his value specifications; he contrasts occupations in terms of their likelihood to satisfy his values; and he receives work samples representative of tasks in occupations of interest to him. Using test and other background data, the prediction component informs the student about his probability for success in specific occupations and helps him to use such actuarial data to make his own decisions. The planning component then guides the student to specify the steps necessary for reaching an occupational goal, and it enables him to explore various alternate strategies for reaching his goals.

Educational Testing Service supplies the special computer and programs for SIGI. It is estimated that the maximum cost of SIGI will be six dollars per hour if a college uses the computer 1,200 hours a year. Currently, Mercer County Community College, New Jersey is using and evaluating the effectiveness of SIGI.

IMPLICATIONS FOR THE COUNSELOR

The seven career counseling procedures described and reviewed in this chapter were all designed to facilitate career choice. From the limited data available concerning the validity of the seven procedures, one can conclude that each has helped some clients in learning how to make career choices. Consequently, each merits consideration for use by the junior college counselor.

All of the procedures, however, need to be investigated more thoroughly, and it is hoped that the descriptions provided in this report will encourage counselors to research the procedures as they use them. Among the unanswered questions of special interest to junior college counselors is whether some procedures are more effective than others in facilitating specific choices or in developing decision-making skills. Whether particular procedures are more appropriate for some populations than for others is also questioned. Inspection of the procedures suggests, for example, that the Williamson, or trait factor procedure, is more likely to assist a client in choosing a specific training program or occupation than in helping him to develop decision-making skills. Ryan simulation procedure effectiveness, however, would be the reverse. Likewise, one might hypothesize that the case-study procedure is more suitable for a group of verbal people, with multiple experiences than for young students from disadvantaged backgrounds. Implicit in the procedure is the assumption that a client will be able to organize and communicate his life's experiences in a verbal format. On the other hand, the Ryan reinforcement procedure appears more suitable to disadvantaged students because its counseling process includes assisting and encouraging the client to assemble and then interpret data relevant to his career decisions. The procedure does not assume that he will be able to do this without help. For counselor assistance and study, a section on methods and instruments for assessing career development has been included in Chapter 5.

CHAPTER 3

COUNSELING PROCEDURES FOR RESOLVING DEFICITS IN VOCATIONAL DEVELOPMENT

THIS CHAPTER PRESENTS six counseling procedures designed primarily to help clients with vocational problems arising from deficits in development. They are not intended to aid occupational selection. The procedures include Roger's client-centered counseling, discovery group counseling, Sorenson's guided inquiry counseling, Bates' (1971) time management counseling, placement skills counseling, and the Holland (1971) Self-Directed Search inventory (SDS). All of the procedures except discovery groups and SDS can be used with individuals or groups. Discovery groups utilize group dynamics while SDS is an individual self-administering inventory.

Each of the procedures has different goals. Client-centered counseling facilitates setting goals and making plans by helping a person accept himself. Discovery groups provide models and marshall group support to encourage clients to achieve their aspirations. The purpose of time management counseling is to assist clients in learning how to organize their time for greater efficiency. Guided inquiry counseling assists a client to resolve a specific problem and achieve a definite goal by leading him through the steps of problem solving. Many different problems can be treated by the procedure as long as the client focuses on one problem at a time. The aim of placement skills counseling is to help clients to develop the skills needed for obtaining a job. The SDS furnishes a list of occupations in which the incumbents have interests and experiences that are similar to those of the client.

These six procedures are particularly appropriate for special junior college subgroups such as homemakers, disadvantaged students, and adults changing occupations. In addition to the typical developmental tasks of junior college, members of these groups often have career problems stemming from interruptions in their work or education or from a failure to make at least horizontal occupational progress.

Homemakers entering college are establishing new identities. To be successful, many must reallocate their time to accommodate new responsibilities. They must accept that college has equal priority with homemaking and educate the family about their reduced accessibility. Concurrently, the homemaker has to develop confidence in her ability to handle new and old roles, to identify her assets and begin focusing on goals which are satisfying and attainable, and to refurbish or aquire the basic academic skills necessary for college.

Disadvantaged persons are also forging new identities. Their lack of models, inadequate preparation, limited parental and peer support, and their unfamiliarity with the mores of the junior college require that they identify goals and subgoals which can be quickly rewarding (Ausubel, 1969). They need to develop confidence when coping with the academic challenges of the community college, develop basic study skills and work habits, control their allocation of time, and educate family and friends about their new responsibilities. A survey of junior colleges indicated that special counseling for the disadvantaged usually comes through federally funded Economic Opportunity Programs, study skills programs, and more intensive exposure to traditional guidance services. Peer and professional counseling in these programs suffer the same lack of replicability characteristic of other counseling. There are several well-developed study skills programs, however, in such colleges as Modesto Junior College, Ulster County Community College, and Des Moines Area Community College.

Adults changing occupations must maintain rather than change their identities as workers. Adults have been economically independent, have produced goods or services by using tested skills, have become accustomed to making their own decisions, and have worked with people whose values and concerns are similar to their own. In order to maintain their identity in college, adults have to reorganize their time commitments, plan in cooperation with their family to live on reduced incomes (Farmer and Williams, 1971), and utilize an environment and services organized to meet adolescent concerns.

Unfortunately, procedures are not available for all career problems. In the presentation of each procedure, recommendations are made about subgroups for which the procedure appears particularly appropriate. Five of the six procedures are described from the perspective of the model of replicable counseling presented in Chapter 1. SDS is an inventory, and consequently its structure and validity are discussed in a different manner.

CLIENT CENTERED COUNSELING

Client-centered counseling has evolved as a method of assisting nonpsychotic persons in resolving various difficulties. It is based on the premise that a counselor can help his clients meet life's challenges by attending and accepting them fully, rather than trying to teach ideas. The counselor limits his instruction to modeling deliberation and acceptance. Counseling is structured to be an experience in which the client can examine his actions and goals in a self-accepting way. Rogers (1951) hypothesizes that such an examination frees a person to set realizable goals and to use his potential for their accomplishment. In order to achieve a self-accepting examination, Rogers hypothesizes that the client must experience acceptance and understanding from another person.

Although research suggests that the procedure would help people with limited confidence to make and implement career plans, the literature does not indicate that client-centered counseling has been used extensively for such a purpose. Consequently, the counselor responses for creating the atmosphere in which a client can grow are described in detail below. Unlike the other procedures described in the monograph, client-centered counseling does not employ specific exercises. Instead, a client's progress is measured by his willingness to accept elements of his situation. Therefore the following description of the procedure focuses on what the client is to do and how the counselor responds to facilitate client movement.

METHOD. Counseling usually begins with a simple invitation to the client to discuss his concern. Thus from the very outset of counseling the client learns that he is responsible for examining his goals and concerns. Hopefully, the client proceeds to present his thoughts and feelings, and, as his trust of counseling increases, his presentation should reveal the unclear aspects of his situation and the feelings and actions which he is unable to accept. With the help of the counselor, the client progresses by the clarification of that which is unclear, by the acceptance of his own feelings and actions, and by either the incorporation or the change of these feelings. Rogers (1951) hypothesizes that a person willingly takes responsibility for his actions as he accepts himself. The stages[1] through which the client will hopefully progress are summarized below:

1. The client talks only about externals and does not recognize a desire to change.
2. The client does not feel responsible for his problem nor does he recognize the feelings which he expresses.
3. The client is able to discuss himself as an object.
4. The client begins to accept his present feelings although he still regards them as objects.
5. The client expresses his feelings more freely, and he indicates a desire to be those feelings.
6. The client's present feelings are expressed directly and immediately.
7. There is a growing trust and openness so that new feelings are accepted immediately. (Rogers, 1961)

Action is the client's, rather than the counselor's, responsibility throughout the sessions. The principal task of the counselor in client-centered counseling is to relate to his client. He reserves judgment and attends exclusively to the client, wishing only to communicate that he will listen. In every session he listens and watches calmly and unhurriedly. He waits for the client to communicate, allowing the client to complete his communication

---

[1] Most clients will progress only two or three steps; it would be remarkable for a client to go from stage one to stage seven through counseling.

before asking a question. Like Williamson, he models deliberation, and, periodically, he paraphrases what the client is saying to be sure that he is understanding the client. When communication is unclear, he notes the need for clarification, and he joins with the client in trying to verbalize the essence of the total communication, including words, tone, and gestures. He tries to respond to the client, rather than provide a program to stimulate him, although data, accumulated by Truax (1966), shows that the client-centered counselor uses reinforcement systematically, suggesting that he is encouraging a problem-solving orientation for his client.

Rogers (1946), Patterson (1966), and Grummon (1972) have indicated that client-centered counseling might encompass components for information dissemination and skills development, even though the client-centered counselors have not usually taught skills or given information. If information on testing is presented during client-centered counseling, Patterson cautioned that the tests be interpreted objectively rather than evaluatively. His example of an objective interpretation is, "three out of four persons with test scores like yours do not complete college." His example of an evaluative interpretation is, "with such a score you should not attend college."

VALIDITY. Client-centered counseling assumes that human growth will occur naturally if the person can accept himself for what he is. It further assumes that problems in self-acceptance occur because significant people in his life have taught the person that part of him is unacceptable (Rogers, 1951). Thus, counseling aims to help the client to correct such mislearning. There is considerable support for the proposition that a person's sense of esteem influences his behavior (Korman, 1970), and several theorists in addition to Rogers theorize that having low esteem stems from relations with parental figures (Adler, 1927; Sullivan, 1953).

Client-centered techniques and counseling have been applied to a wide range of human concerns (Grummon, 1971), and extensive research indicates that the key elements of this approach—counselor communication, empathy, and positive regard

—relate to growth in counseling (Truax and Carkhuff, 1967). Insofar as career problems are concerned, findings by Bartlett (1949) and Healy, et al. (1973) suggest that client-centered counseling might assist persons who are having difficulty adjusting to work demands and difficulty making appropriate career choices.

In the UCLA survey that provides much of the information reported here, junior college counselors indicated that they used some Rogerian techniques in their career counseling. Bert Anderson described the guidelines for group counseling at Modesto college which incorporates much of the client-centered procedure. They appear in Table II.

TABLE II

GUIDELINES FOR GROUP COUNSELING AT
MODESTO JUNIOR COLLEGE

When Listening:

1. You are to hear each other. Concentrate on understanding the *Feelings* of the person who is sharing.

2. Listen with acceptance, openness, and *Positive Interest*. Withhold judgment or advice.

3. Please *Check Back* with the other person until *He* feels that you understand his point of view and feelings.

4. Encourage others to attend to their feelings and share them with the group, but don't pry or prod.

5. Always listen with *Care and Concern*.

When Sharing:

1. Be honest with yourself—tune in to your own feelings so that you can share them with the group.

2. Be specific and personal.

3. Aim your sharing toward the whole group, not just to one person.

4. You may be confident that others will listen to you, try to understand you, accept what you have to say, and respect it as true for you.

DISCOVERY GROUPS

Discovery or consciousness-raising groups are becoming popular throughout the country. Insofar as they utilize group dynamics, they offer great promise for helping clients define and pursue their goals. Two consciouness-raising procedures, Human Potential Counseling and Life Planning Workshops, have already proved helpful to persons when making and implementing careers. Both of these procedures are described in detail.

The two procedures are comprised of group exercises in which the clients discuss their aspirations and problems in a supportive setting and, in turn, support others in doing the same. The procedures rely upon client modeling and group reinforcement of the modeled behavior. The descriptions of the exercises focus on what clients do. Only minimal attention is paid to the role of the counselor. In each procedure, however, the counselor's role appears to be similar. He describes the exercises and regulates pace, while facilitating participation. These procedures do not indicate the indices to use in judging when an exercise should end, techniques for involving clients in the exercises, or whether a counselor should employ such devices as the redirected or open-end question. Problem solving techniques for clients who are not complying with the exercise are not discussed, nor do the procedures generally specify rules for using reinforcement.

HUMAN POTENTIAL COUNSELING. Otto (1966) developed several procedures to help persons feel capable of setting and achieving goals. One of his procedures, termed the Multiple Strength Perception Method, has been adapted by Trueblood, McHolland (1970), and Quirck at Ulster Community College to help educationally disadvantaged students set educational and vocational goals. In the adaptations, each client is given the experience of publicly setting short term goals with the commitment to report his progress to the group. Participation is voluntary and clients are helped to understand their role in counseling before they begin.

At the first session, clients get acquainted with each other and are oriented to the objectives and activities of counseling. A get-acquainted component like that used in the Healy procedure (Chapter 2) should be used to help clients learn more about each other. Counseling requires good understanding between clients. Indeed, Otto (1968) uses strength bombardment only after clients are sufficiently acquainted. This maintains "minimal latent hostility." After becoming acquainted, clients are told about goal setting which they are expected to do at the close of each session. Progress reports are given at subsequent sessions. They are taught that goals should be: describable, believable by the person setting them, achievable within a week, measurable, desirable, and specific. Over the course of counseling, clients are urged to set ever more challenging goals and to report their progress in the counseling session.

Subsequent sessions begin with the counselor's description of an exercise. He then focuses on a selected client, enabling other clients to carry out the exercise. The order in which clients become the central focus of the group is determined by drawing lots. Sessions last for one and one-fourth to two hours, although Otto has indicated that the strength bombardment exercise can take forty minutes per client. Quirck reports that groups of twelve to fifteen take two to three sessions per exercise. Each group of clients experiences the exercises in the following order: "strength bombardment," "success bombardment," and "discussion of values." The objectives and content of each exercise are discussed below.

The strength bombardment exercise is designed to enable a person to experience, in a positive way, the realization and utilization of personal strengths. Each client in his turn describes strengths such as—"mechanical," "strong," "good talker," etc.—and, then, asks the group to relate the attributes they see in him. Usually, the group adds strengths he has not mentioned (Otto, 1968). Following this, the client asks the group to tell what they feel is preventing him from using his good points to better advantage—to describe his weaknesses. During interaction with the client, group members may ask for information related to the client's strengths and weaknesses, but the individual is not asked to enumerate his weaknesses.

The intent of the exercise is to bombard the client with the positive rather than to recall weaknesses. However, in order to prevent the client from feeling that a non-existent person is being discussed, it appears important to insure that weaknesses which he regards as major are not ignored. Accordingly, it is recommended that the counselor ask a client whether he has additional weaknesses whenever the group appears to omit one. After the client's characteristics are identified, the counselor asks the group to relate their dream about what the client would be like in five or ten years if he were using all his strengths. After hearing the predictions of his fellows, the client shares his feelings about his strength bombardment.

The success bombardment is intended to help a client become aware of his success pattern, the differences in his success and non-success experiences, and the areas in which he has not investigated his potential. When his name is drawn, the client tells the groups about his three most successful experiences, such as "winning a sporting event," "earning a grade," etc. Then he describes three recent experiences in which he was unsuccessful. The group questions him to determine whether he was doing something when he was successful that he was not doing when he was unsuccessful. For example, the group might help the client to discover that his success in a track meet came after long, hard practice, while failure in an English test occurred because of minimal preparation.

The discussion of values enables the client to clarify and acknowledge his values and gain peer acceptance. Clients are helped, for example, to feel that they can want to help people, be financially comfortable, be good students, etc., and still be accepted. In order to begin the exercise, each client, in turn, tells the group his three most important values. (Quirck hangs cards with the names of different positive values in the counseling room.) The group reinforces his values by asking him to clarify the meanings. In this exercise, the client is helped by relating values to strengths and goals; he will, thus, realize how they fit together.

Life Planning Workshops. The Counseling Center at Colorado State University has developed an all day workshop consisting of seven discussion exercises to help college students and other adults clarify and identify their life roles and realize their ability and responsibility for choosing the direction of their lives.

The workshop leader explains the roles and divides the participants into groups of four relative strangers and one facilitator. Facilitators are former clients who have completed the seven exercises. The workshop leader urges the clients "to act as consultants to one another and to intervene, reflect, probe, and even push to help others examine their future." The purpose and content of the seven exercises are presented below.

Life line is an exercise intended to encourage the person to focus on what will happen, rather than concentrating on what has happened. Persons draw a line on a piece of paper, label one half "past" and one half "future." They then write their thoughts about past and future and proceed to discuss the future, giving only minimal attention to their history.

Identification and Stripping of Roles is designed to help clients "recognize the influence of specific roles on their lives and on their future plans." This enables them to "experience the remainder of the exercises free of the influence of their role."[1] The clients lists his significant roles, spouse, student, etc., in the order of their importance; he then "strips" his roles one at a time and discusses his feelings about giving up each role. After all roles are relinquished, the client fantasizes about himself without the roles, sharing his feelings. In the course of role divesture, individuals are expected to learn how certain roles are in conflict with their plans.

The Typical Day and Special Day of the Future exercise requires the client to describe himself on a typical and on a special day in the future. Subsequent discussions of each client's days are intended to distinguish the realistic from idealistic, to pinpoint inconsistences, and to examine ways in which the goals might be realized. After the exercise, the client should be more able to consider his roles in terms of his own wants.

The Life Inventory Exercise requires the client to specify, in answer to a series of questions, the things that he would like to do differently and the things that he does well. Discussion is intended to help him make plans consistent with his assets and newly formulated goals.

The News Release Exercise requires the person to forecast what his major roles, accomplishments, and pleasures will be at some future time, in the form of a news release for a home town paper. Group discussion examines how and whether the individual is moving toward such goals.

In the *Reassume Roles Exercise*, each client either reassumes his old roles, or substitutes more desirable roles, and he announces

---

[1] The authors warn users to insure that clients are psychologically able to engage in this exercise before allowing them to participate.

the roles he has selected. The client can substitute roles or he can rearrange the priority of old roles. This exercise is intended to accentuate the changes he is planning to make and to provide him with a sense of control in making decisions about his future.

Goals Setting is the final exercise. Each client lists specific behaviors which he can perform immediately, or in the near future, to direct him toward his goals. Group discussion focuses on reinforcing the clients' commitment to acting to achieve the goals that he has elected.

VALIDITY. The validity of each of the discovery procedures depends in part upon whether they elicit career obstacles that are relevant for the individual as well as strategies that are sufficiently specific and realistic for achieving goals and resolving problems. Otto (1968) found that in his strength bombardment exercise, group members typically identify several strengths which the client had not named himself. However, research has not yet examined the relative stimulus value of Otto's other exercises or of the exercises of the Life Planning Workshop. Research is needed, for example, to show that instructions describe a typical day in the future, free of the restraints of current roles, enables most people to write descriptions that are sufficiently realistic and specific to be helpful when setting goals and anticipating problems.

Limited, direct research on the effects of the two procedures has been supportive. Otto (1966) reported that his procedure strengthened the self-image and enhanced the confidence of participants, although he did not report statistical data supporting his observations. Trueblood and McHolland (1970) reported that thirty-three educationally disadvantaged college freshmen who received Human Potential Counseling increased their self-regard and became more self-directing on the *Personal Orientation Inventory* (Shostram, 1963) than sixty-six similar students who were not counseled. Birney, Thomas, and Hinkle (1970) found that forty clients increased their self-regard and self-understanding, reduced their anxiety, and felt other people were more meaningful after participating in life planning workshops.

At Ulster County Community College, the combination of

Human Potential Counseling and a remedial study program has improved academic motivation, willingness to speak in groups and share concerns, and clarity of goals. At Phoenix College, Emil Kass reported that human potential techniques have been integrated into the career planning course, resulting in increased student satisfaction, especially among adults. In 1972-73, it was anticipated that there would be twenty-four sections of the planning course. The Phoenix College program includes exercises in sharing a positive experience, relaxation training, cooperative puzzle assembly without talking, practice in listening to others, sharing reaction to one's interest test results, strength bombardment, and role playing of situations of interest to the clients.

At the University of Minnesota Extension, Mannis and Mochizuki (1972) have constructed a discovery procedure which has assisted home-makers in giving each other support, building self-confidence and self-awareness, returning to college, obtaining employment, and locating suitable volunteer activities.

REPLICABILITY. The discovery procedures were not designed to meet a criterion of replicability. However, since the experiences are clearly described and their goals are specified, or can readily be inferred, they can be replicable if the counselor specifies some exercises in greater detail, uses standardized procedures in acquainting clients with their roles in counseling, and employs a defined repertoire of responses. In exercises such as strength bombardment, for example, the counselor needs to specify the range of characteristics from which strengths and weaknesses are to be drawn to be able to pace counseling in a uniform way. To do this, the counselor might specify and, either directly or by modeling, inform the client that the exercise is complete only after the group has focused on the client's school and nonschool activities, his demeanor and appearance in presenting his strengths, and his participation in identifying skills of other group members. Likewise, since the effectiveness of the procedure is dependent upon the active participation of group members and since there are several methods of eliciting such participation which differ in effectiveness, the counselor must specify which he will use. To date, research suggests that video and live client models are the most effective methods for developing such participation (Bandura, 1969). Finally, the counselor needs to define a response repertoire in a manner similar to that described in Chapter 1. The authors of discovery procedures do not define such a repertoire.

GUIDED INQUIRY COUNSELING

In an effort to increase client options through acquaintance with the benefits of utilizing behavioral science principles to resolve problems, Sorenson and his students (1967, 1968) are developing a method of counseling they term the guided inquiry method. In this procedure, the client is guided through the four phases of problem solving by a Socratic questioning technique; the counselor uses cueing and open-ended questions to help a client: (1) to identify his goals in terms of what he and others would be doing and to specify what is currently preventing him from realizing his goal; (2) to recall or discover alternative strategies for correcting what is happening and review the consequences of applying each of the alternative strategies; (3) to choose a strategy and plan to carry it out; and (4) to report his efforts and either continue to apply a successful strategy or recycle the phases of problem solving. The procedure is designed for all types of problems, but it has been found especially helpful in such career conflicts as difficulties with one's supervisor or peers, difficulty in learning job skills, confusion about a career decision, etc. A detailed description of the phases through which the counselor leads the client follows.

METHOD. The Guided Inquiry procedure is replicable but not standardized. Each client is guided through the same phases of problem solving (Table III), but their content depends on the client's problem and his understanding of behavioral science principles. Counselors model a calm, deliberative problem solving approach, and they use a uniform repertoire of responses. Each client eventually specifies his goals, his obstacles, and strategies in terms of behaviors at definite times and places. However, every client has his own goals, obstacles, and strategies, and any two clients may use different behavioral science principles to accomplish similar goals. For example, two students may be concerned about their inability to get along with their laboratory instructor (LI) and their consequent inability to profit from his supervision. The counselor helps each to define his goal as correcting deficiencies in his lab procedures identified by the LI. One student, however, discovers that his many questions make the instructor anxious. The other realizes that he is encouraging the instructor to tell him only about the negative aspects of his laboratory efforts in their conferences, resulting in dejected, angry feelings. In the first case, the student needs to recall or discover that making another person anxious reduces his ability to relate; in the second case, the student must recognize that by establishing the instructor as a punitive figure, he is insuring that he will not relate well to him. Consequently, the replicability of the procedure depends not upon a predetermined content but upon completing the same phases, defining goals, obstacles and solutions with the same specificity, and experiencing the same class of counselor response. Table III outlines the phases of the guided inqury procedure; they are described in detail below.

In phase 1 of this method, the counselor helps the client with three objectives: (1) To feel that the counselor is interested in him and concerned about his needs; (2) to accurately describe his beliefs about his problem and its place in his life; and (3)

TABLE III

FOUR PHASES OF GUIDED INQUIRY COUNSELING

Phase 1	Develop picture of person Explain how counseling will help Specify goal Specify obstacles Summarize
Phase 2	Relate obstacles to behavioral science concepts Identify solution strategies Delineate consequences of each strategy Summarize
Phase 3	Choose one strategy for implementation Plan for implementation Summarize
Phase 4	Report on strategy trial Continue with, or modify strategy or recycle to Phase 1 Summarize

to state his problem in terms of specific situations and obstacles. He accomplishes his first two objectives by listening attentively and nonjudgmentally as he guides his client in the description of what he believes are his concerns, how he feels about them, what he believes cause them, what he believes should be done about them, and what he has already tried to do.

Open-ended questions, paraphrasing, reflection of feeling, and expectant silence are used to help the client describe himself and the impact of his problem. For example, the student having difficulty with the laboratory instructor might be asked questions such as, "What happens between you and Mr. X" . . . You are feeling frustration in trying to resolve it? . . . What impact is this having on your other studies, social life, etc.? . . . What might explain why you are not getting along with him? . . . Oh, you have hunches about resolving the problem! . . . And what happened when you tried that?"

To accomplish the third objective, the counselor asks the client open-ended and cueing questions in an attempt to help him say what he wants to occur, what is preventing it from happening, and what goals should be sought first. Once the client identifies the specific goal and its obstacles, the counselor guides the client to summarize his understanding of what they will be doing. Counseling then moves to the second phase.

The objectives of phase 2 are to help the client recall or learn alternate strategies for overcoming the obstacles he specified in phase 1. He should also review the probable consequences of each strategy. The counselor first poses questions about the occurrence of the obstacle so the client can clarify the cause, especially his part in it. For example, the student who was making the instructor anxious would be asked such questions as: "What occurs before you feel you cannot relate to him? . . . What does he do? . . . What do you do? . . . What appears to be constant in the meetings in which you are not relating well?"

Once the client has delineated one or more probable causes, the counselor questions him about strategies for removing, preventing, or circumventing each obstacle. (In deciding when to accept a cause as probable and consequently, when to proceed to

Counseling Procedures for Resolving Deficits

consider alternate solution strategies, the counselor relies on his understanding of the problem area. This understanding comes from his own study of such problems and his past experience.) After noting that the instructor was anxious in their conferences, the student in our example would be asked such questions as: "How might you prevent the instructor from becoming anxious? . . . Might you rehearse your questions before conferring with him in order to avoid arousing his anxiety? . . . Are there times at which he is less likely to be anxious? . . . What principles about anxiety might be helpful in suggesting ways to proceed? . . . For example, do you recall that people become anxious when they are asked questions which they cannot answer, and that one person can generate calm or anxiety in another by being calm or anxious? . . . What approach do such principles suggest? . . ."

After the client specifies several strategies, the counselor guides him into considering the requirements and probable consequences of each strategy. In the case of the student who specifies the strategy of relaxing by listening to soft music before conferring with his instructor, the counselor asks about the probable consequences and the principles which can help the student to predict them. The counselor might ask: "If you are calm and ask few questions, what will happen? . . . What makes you think so? . . . What will you have to do in order to be calm and ask few questions?" As the phase closes, the counselor or client summarizes the strategies which have been recalled or discovered. To the student in the example, the counselor might say: "You believe that you can reduce the instructor's anxiety in several ways: (1) By being calm and asking few questions when you confer, (2) By scheduling conferences when he is unlikely to be anxious."

In phase 3, the counselor guides the client into committing himself to act, to report that action, and to evaluate the action. First the counselor asks the client which strategy he is going to try and its probability of success in comparison with other possible strategies. He then leads the client into the delineation of the steps he will take when using the strategy. With the example, of the student, the counselor may ask such questions as: "What are you going to do to relax before your conference? . . . How are you going to stop yourself from asking questions? . . . Are you going to rehearse the previous night?" The counselor's instructional repertoire is not limited to discovery; he can teach skills like relaxation or give information didactically.

The counselor next asks the client about the criteria he will use for evaluating his success. In the example of the student, he would be asked about signs which would indicate that the instructor's anxiety diminishes during their conferences. In addition, he will be reminded to distinguish reduced anxiety from receiving constructive feedback, since it is only his hypothesis that anxiety is preventing the instructor from giving feedback. Thus, the student might be asked: "How will you know whether the instructor is less anxious during your conference? . . . How will you know whether you are following your plan? . . ."

After the client chooses a strategy and defines the steps and indices by which to determine its success, the counselor asks him to review what he will be doing. He closes the session by reminding the client that they can discuss the outcome of the strategy at the next meeting.

The objectives of phase 4 are that the client report the results of his actions and either modify the strategy, continue with it, or select a new one. If a new strategy is required, the counselor recycles phases 1, 2 and 3, adding the data which the client has acquired from trying a strategy. If the client has been unable to apply the strategy, he and the counselor determine the reason and then add corrective measures to the steps of the strategy. For example, if the student failed to carry out his plan because he talked to the instructor right after a competitive game, he would be asked to state ways by which he could avoid such interference in the future.

When the client is successful, the counselor encourages him to describe his success and his feelings about it, and he asks the client to review how he can proceed in the future so that successs continues. The counselor and the client then decide whether to continue counseling to resolve other problems or to terminate counseling with this session.

The rationale of the Guided Inquiry procedure includes the

assumption that individuals can be more effective problem solvers if they apply solutions based upon psychological principles, an assumption that is implicit in all counseling which can be described as teaching (London, 1964). The actual procedure follows Gaynë's (1970) steps of problem solving.

Guided Inquiry Counseling has been studied in several doctoral dissertations at UCLA. It has been used successfully to help student teachers relate more effectively with supervisors (Quinn, 1971), to reduce the anxiety of student teaching assignments (Sorenson & Hawkins, 1968), and to learn techniques of teaching (Farmer, 1972). Although Sorenson's procedure has not been used extensively, it is a potentially valuable tool for assisting junior college students with a wide range of problems. For example, disadvantaged youth who feel isolated on campus could be guided to discover strategies for winning friends, and adults and homemakers could be assisted in developing methods for coping with the stresses in the interpersonal relations that arise with their new student responsibilities.

BATES' TIME MANAGEMENT COUNSELING

When examining difficulties disadvantaged persons were having implementing career plans, Sorenson hypothesized that many problems arose because such persons had not developed habits, i.e. time management, perseverance, etc., that were conducive to success. In accord with such an hypothesis, Bates designed a procedure which helped veterans from disadvantaged homes to better regulate their class and work routines. It has long been realized that one must be able to regulate his time to accomplish career tasks (Robinson, 1946; Shartle, 1959). (Many manuals for time scheduling are available.) However, Bates is one of the few authors who has constructed a counseling procedure utilizing group dynamics and modeling to assist in achieving the goal of improved time management and, consequently, the exercises and counselors responses of her procedure are described here in detail.

In the procedure, each client learns a time planning model, methods of rewarding himself, and strategies for coping with obstacles to effective time management. Emphasizing systematic problem solving principles and the use of open-ended and cue questions, the counselor assumes more of a didactic teaching than discovery learning role. He arranges conditions so that students with reported deficits in time management can learn new approaches to handle their time. The counselor introduces each session's topic, summarizes past sessions, lectures, gives written exercises and homework, demonstrates exercises, gives a written performance test after every session, and thanks each client as he hands it in. There are nine one-hour sessions, each of which has its own incremental subgoals. The goals and content of each session are described below.

METHOD. In session 1, each client: (1) learns the group's purpose; (2) identifies potential benefits of improving his time management; (3) defines and (4) gives examples of study skills and work habits, and defines time management. To accomplish the first two objectives, the counselor states the purpose of the group meetings and the advantages of time management, answers client questions, and asks each student to relate his ideas about the value of time management. In order to accomplish objectives three and four, the counselor solicits definitions and examples of studying, learning, and study skill as well as examples of obstacles to studying, such as T.V. viewing, "rapping," etc. Next, ways of eliminating obstacles are explored, and then the counselor summarizes the major points and definitions of the session, elicits client recommendations for improving counseling, and administers the performance test on the session's content.

In session 2, clients learn about the time planning model and its three parts. After reviewing session 1 and clarifying mistakes on the performance test, the counselor describes time planning and distributes a Master Time Plan. (Appendix G) His questions guide the client to discover that such a plan lists the days of the week and the fixed activities for the hours of those days. Next, he encourages each client to fill out their own Master Time Plan, and he works with each to correct errors or omissions.

The counselor explains that time planning requires a Master Time Plan, a Hot Sheet, and an Action Plan (Appendix G). The

Master Time Plan is one's fixed schedule; the Hot Sheet is a weekly list of assignments by time priority; and the Action Plan is a list of specific hours for accomplishing tasks on the Hot Sheet. The student receives a copy and an example of each, and he fills them in. The counselor then urges the clients to try their plans, note the time their assignments take, and use blocks of time for their assignments. In closing, he praises those who say that they will try some part of time planning.

The objectives of session 3 are that each client list an Action Plan, incorporate the Action Plan onto the Master Time Plan, commit himself to trying it, and arrange to use idle time between classes productively. After reviewing the major concepts of previous sessions and rewarding clients for trying any part of their plans, the counselor helps the clients to complete their Hot Sheets, giving assistance in such things as deciding priorities among assignments, etc. Clients then inspect their Master Time Plans for times in which to complete class assignments, and they write those times in their Action Plan. Following this, the counselor discusses using idle time in school to review notes, etc., and he asks the clients both to identify such times in their Master Time Plans and to write in productive activities for such hours.

Session 4's objectives are that clients list their assignments for the week, identify and reward those who are trying time planning, and consider ways for overcoming obstacles to time planning. After reviewing previous sessions and the performance test, the clients share their experiences of managing their time. Those who are successful tell how they feel; those who are not, tell their reasons for not trying or describe the obstacles which they have encountered, state ways for overcoming them, and affirm their commitment to try. If these clients cannot name strategies, those who have been successful tell about their methods, and/or the counselor suggests strategies. Time logs receive attention next. The counselor provides sheets for tallying the hours spent in different activities, and the clients identify the activities which consume their time, especially noting the amount of time utilized in studying different subjects. Samples of other students' time usage are reviewed to elicit suggestions about improving time usage, and then, clients critically review their own time logs and identify ways for improving their time usage. The session closes with a clarification of the aspects of time planning which each client will try before the next session.

In session 5, clients learn to reward themselves for productive use of time; that is, they define reward, name rewards which they can use, define task analysis, and tell how task analysis facilitates time management. After reviewing past sessions and client assignments, the counselor then introduces the topic of rewarding oneself. Clients are guided to discover that people act for rewards, and they discuss the applicability of this concept to their lives. They distinguish external from internal rewards and name rewards which they can use, such as meeting a challenge, "rapping" with friends, etc.

The counselor then suggests that they can study more efficiently by giving themselves small rewards, a cup of coffee, a telephone call, etc., for accomplishing their assignments, and rewards are more effective when they are frequent and come soon after completion of an assignment. This information leads into the need to divide study assignments into blocks which can be rewarded frequently. To demonstrate such task analysis, the counselor guides the group through an analysis of an upcoming assignment. Following that, every client lists assignments for which he will reward himself.

In session 6, clients learn about a continuum of steps for achieving time management, identify obstacles and corresponding solutions ,and define "distributed study." After the clients have reported their time management efforts, the counselor introduces the concept of a set of steps for achieving time management. The steps range over activities like coming to counseling, filling out and then adhering to each of the time planning forms, estimating the time requirements of activities, and designating specific blocks of time for long range assignments. The counselor explains why each is a distinct step, points out the advantage of doing one step at a time, and helps each client to locate his next step. Clients then discuss why they have not taken their next step and how they might accomplish it. Finally, distributed study is presented as a method of improving study efficiency by increasing incidental learning and decreasing fatigue. The counselor provides examples of distributed study and guides the students' application of the concept of their situation through appropriate cue questions.

In session 7, the client learns to define coping strategy and names some which he can try. After reviewing past sessions and checking completion of past assignments, the counselor initiates discussion of coping strategy by recalling the obstacles which had been interfering with the clients' planning. The counselor insures that "coping strategy" is defined, and that strategies, such as "remove distractions from study area and start studying according to schedule regardless of mood," are discussed by distributing a sheet of distractors and strategies for coping with them. At the close of the session, clients complete their Hot Sheets for the following week and are urged to try the strategies for realizing their plans.

Session 8's objectives include client identification of the remaining steps to be accomplished for effective management of time. The client must learn ways of making school subjects interesting. While clients report their progress in following the time plan model at the start of the session, each is helped to identify the steps which he has not taken and to commit himself to these. Next, the counselor initiates discussion on the topic of developing interest in courses. This is done by stating that people can improve their school performance by developing such interest. In the discussion, clients are guided to generate a list of principles, such as "Ask friends who enjoy apparently dull classes their reasons for liking them." "Review a subject in a more elementary textbook in order to understand it, etc."

The objective of session 9, the final session, is to evaluate whether the clients have learned the major concepts in time planning and if they are using them. The counselor asks the clients to complete the planning forms without assistance and then asks each about the elements of time planning which he has tried.

VALIDITY AND REPLICABILITY. Bates followed Gagné's (1970) problem solving approach for developing time management counseling from the study skills programs of Robinson (1946) and Pauk (1962). To validate the procedure, thirty-eight Viet

Nam veterans enrolled in a special UCLA Extension program to develop academic skills completed, the procedure and their results were compared with thirty-eight matched controls. Bates found that the thirty-eight counseled veterans reduced their unproductive use of time, tried more assignments, and felt better able to manage time than the thirty-eight controls. In a replication study, Vivell (1972) found that the Bates' procedure helped thirty-two black 12th graders increase their study skills and grades. Although the procedure has been used only with persons of disadvantaged academic or social backgrounds and focuses on accomplishing school assignments, this procedure appears appropriate for homemakers and other adults changing careers who must fit new responsibilities into their life schedules.

To insure replicabiilty, Bates constructed a script which prescribed appropriate counselor behavior. An excerpt of the script appears in Appendix H. In the Bates study, two raters agreed that counselors performed according to script 95 percent of the time. In Vivell's study, two raters judged that the counselors adhered to the script at least 92 percent of the time, with a median of 95 percent.

SELF DIRECTED SEARCH

Holland's Self Directed Search (SDS) is an inventory which, by eliciting a client's experiences and preferences, directs him without counselor assistance to occupations whose members have interests and competencies similar to his. SDS is included in this review of replicable counseling procedures because it is designed to substitute for, rather than merely supplement, the self and occupational exploration components of career counseling. Other inventories, particularly the Kuder Vocational Preference Record (1948), might be used in a similar fashion, but their authors have not suggested nor tested their potential. Holland and his colleagues, on the other hand, are testing the hypothesis that the SDS will substitute for a counselor. In the following pages, the inventory is described and research pertinent to it is reviewed.

Self-administered and self-scored, the SDS provides a standardized situation in which the client answers questions about his likes, achievements, and preferences for carefully selected activities and occupations. Each item belongs to one of six scales that represent Holland's (1959) six personality types—realistic, intellectual, conventional, enterprising, social, and artistic. The client tabulates his score for each scale, follows an arithmetic procedure for weighting different scale items, and derives his three highest scale scores in an hierarchial order. These scores comprise his occupational code; that is, if his highest score were realistic, (R), his second highest intellectual (I), and his third highest artistic (A), his occupational code would by RIA. After deriving his own code, the client compares it to the codes of 495 occupations which employ about 95 percent of the labor force in the United States. These 495 occupational codes were determined by empirical and logical analysis (Holland, Viernstein, Kuo, Karweit, and Blum, 1970).

The SDS takes a client through a personal inventory of his likes and competencies, thereby furnishing him with a model of systematic introspection which might be helpful in the future occupational choices he can expect to make. Although no effort has been made to encourage the client to complete such an inventory in the future, SDS might become such a model by alerting the client to the benefits of such an inventory whenever one is contemplating an occupational choice.

There are no counselor responses for SDS. Its completion, however, is expected to stimulate some clients to seek counseling assistance to locate occupations for exploration and resolve conflicts, such as discrepancies between perceived and inventoried similarities in jobs, unearthed by SDS (Holland, 1971). If a client should seek help, the manual suggests only that the counselor verify that his calculations are correct, and that he obtain additional information. For replicability with clients who seek counselor help after using SDS, however, guidelines are needed which prescribe the steps a counselor will use in helping such clients obtain additional information or resolve conflicts.

VALIDITY AND REPLICABILITY. The occupational leads furnished by SDS are based upon findings from Holland's (1966) extensive research of occupational personality types. Holland (1971) has found that students and adults generally feel that these leads are accurate. In the one direct study of SDS's effectiveness as a form of counseling, Zenner and Schnuelle (1972) found that completion of SDS in contrast to no counseling increased the number of occupations that a client was considering, increased his certainty and satisfaction with his preferences, and increased the probability that his occupational preference was consistent with his inventoried interests and competencies. In addition, completion of SDS decreased requests for vocational counseling but did not increase requests for specific occupational information.

Several studies have shown that the SDS codes are as reliable as other interest inventory scores, thereby indicating that the outcome of SDS is relatively replicable. In their study of 1,092 high school students, Zenner and Schnuelle found that the rank order of the six Holland scales had a median test-retest reliability of .82. In another study, O'Connell and Sedlacek (1971) found a median test-retest correlation of $r=.75$ and Spearman Rho of .92 for 5,000 University of Maryland freshmen. Such reliability data certainly affirm the potential usefulness of SDS.

PLACEMENT SKILLS PROCEDURE

An important task of students and adults alike is securing a job commensurate with their training and career goals. Getting that right job is a crucial step in everyone's career and, consequently, it is not surprising that accomplishing this task creates anxiety in most people. However, it should be surprising that many people approach this crucial task with minimal knowledge of the skills needed to obtain that important job and that replicable counseling procedures for developing such skills have not been reported. Consequently, in the following pages, this author describes role playing and role reversal exercises and counselor responses which the research literature and his experience in placement counseling suggest will be effective.

Role playing and role reversal share similarities but are

different activities. Role playing consists of rehearsing an anticipated interaction with actors to understand and improve one's performance. The client plays himself, and the counselor or other clients play other significant figures in the interaction. Rehearsal permits a client to evaluate and improve actions by practice before entering the real interaction. In addition, the rehearsal experience usually allays anxiety. If designed primarily to reduce anxiety, role playing is frequently preceded by relaxation exercises (Bandura, 1969). In role reversal, the client rehearses the anticipated interaction by playing his protagonist vis-a-vis the counselor or another actor who plays the client. By adopting and experiencing a protagonist's perspective on the interaction and by viewing another's portrayal of him, the client is enabled to develop understanding and skills that can facilitate relating to the protagonist in the real interaction.

Replicable role playing requires that a counselor specify the principles to be learned from role playing, include elements in his scenario which are likely to expose the client to those principles, and use a defined repertoire of responses in guiding the client through the scenario. For example, to teach a job seeker that he must state his qualifications specifically,[2] in role play the counselor can ask such questions as: "In what job can you start? ... What makes you believe that you will be successful with us?" The College Placement Annual lists behaviors that are generally regarded as appropriate for job seeking.

In order to maximize the effectiveness of role playing situations, the counselor should insure that the following occurs: (1) Role players volunteer, after being informed of the purpose of role playing and being alerted to the possibility of exposing aspects of their personality. (2) Role players receive descriptions of the scenario and the people they are to play in sufficient time to study materials and to obtain clarification. Scripts are not generally used. If some members of a counseling group are to be an audience, their role should also be clarified. (3) The

---

[2] The Group Guidance Program of the University of Houston is using role playing as one of its techniques in teaching job seeking skills, and J. A. Pruzak (1969) recently described role playing exercises to develop job seeking skills in use at the Minnesota Rehabilitation Center.

simulated scenario approximates the real situation to the greatest degree possible. For example, if the client is role playing a job interview, the interviewer should be as formidable and as thorough as one would expect an employment interviewer to be. If available, props should also be used. (4) As soon as the role playing is complete, the client shares his reaction about what happened, receives reinforcement and feedback about the positive aspects of his performance, and discusses methods for improving his performance. The counselor insures that each important element of the situation is discussed. (5) The client has the opportunity to repeat his performance after planning corrections in order to be reinforced for improvement, especially if role playing occurs in groups. (6) Role playing is continuous unless the scenario specifically calls for interruptions. The realism of the role playing situation and, consequently, its learning impact can be lost if a player steps in and out of his role. This is especially true in role reversal.

IMPLICATIONS FOR THE COUNSELOR

The procedures reviewed in this chapter have been designed primarily to reduce problems that arise during choosing and in implementing a career, rather than to teach a client how to choose a career. As noted earlier, several subgroups of junior college students can be expected to have special problems in utilizing a junior college to achieve their goals. The procedures described here have been helpful in teaching approaches for resolving some of these problems and, consequently, are worth considering for use in the junior college.

Data about the kind and amount of help which a particular procedure provides, as well as data about the components of a procedure which produce benefit are limited, and more research is obviously needed. For example, client-centered counseling appears to help clients both to specify goals which they feel they can achieve and to resolve communication problems with employers or supervisors. But it may only provide such help to persons who have knowledge about problem solving. Yet, one might hypothesize that the addition of components which develop problem-solving skills would broaden the coverage of the client-centered counseling to persons who lack such skills. Consequently counselors will have to validate the procedures as they use them, and it is expected that the section on methods of measuring career development presented in Chapter 5 will facilitate such study.

CHAPTER 4

OVERVIEW OF THIRTEEN REPLICABLE CAREER COUNSELING PROCEDURES

OUR SURVEY OF the literature, a sampling of 200 community college counseling centers, and conference with 55 counselors from 27 southern California community colleges has revealed 13 replicable counseling procedures. These have been described and reviewed. The thirteen share certain characteristics, are distinguishable in others, and together contain limitations.

At least four similar characteristics are common to the thirteen procedures. First and most important, their replicability indicates that each is a set of defined components with specific goals. As a consequence, every procedure has criteria against which the counselor can assess his counseling as it occurs, and each defines points at which the counselor can assess his client's progress. Information from both assessments will either encourage the counselor to proceed, confident that he is following his plan and that the client is progressing, or it will provide early warning that he needs to either correct his counseling, recycle, or replace a component that has not accomplished its goal. The property of replicability, therefore, increases the potential of a procedure for success. Second, several of the response repertoires can be employed with all procedures. A counselor using the Williamson, client-centered, or guided inquiry procedures, for example, can use the same techniques for involving clients, solving problems, etc. Since a counselor need not vary his response repertoire as he changes procedures, the components of the thirteen procedures can be interchanged without confusing a client. The potential of using identical responses across all procedures means that the counselor who mastered one procedure will be able to master the other twelve relatively easily. Thus, to learn a second procedure, he will have only to familiarize himself with the content of the components peculiar to that new procedure. Third, each procedure assumes that deliberation about problems is helpful; each helps the client to deliberate about who he is and what he wants to become. Each allows the counselor to model reflection and deliberation, reinforces clients for gathering information and planning, and assumes that the examined life is a more successful life. Fourth, each procedure also requires the client to accept responsibility for implementing the plans he makes in counseling. No procedure directs the counselor to intervene with others on behalf of the client. The components of each of the thirteen are designed to stimulate action. Counselors may reward, rehearse, and verify implementation of plans. At no time, however, are they expected to carry out any part of the client's plan.

DIFFERENCES

The differences among the thirteen procedures are summarized in Table IV and are discussed below.

TABLE IV

DIFFERENCE AMONG 13 COUNSELING PROCEDURES

Emphasis	Elements in Counseling	Minimum Emphasis
1, 2, 3, 4, 5, 6, 7, 10, 11, 12, 13	Systematic planning	8, 9
2, 3, 4, 6, 10, 11, 12	reinforcement	1, 5, 7, 8, 9, 13
8, 9, 10	self-acceptance	1, 2, 3, 4, 5, 6, 7, 11, 12, 13
1, 2, 3, 5, 6, 7	Interpretation of empirical/data	4, 8, 9, 10, 11, 13
1, 2, 3, 4, 6, 7, 10, 11	Specificity of problems and goals	5, 8, 9, 12, 13
1, 2, 3, 4, 5, 6, 7, 9, 10, 11	Ongoing evaluation of process	8
2, 3, 4, 5, 8, 10, 11	transferability of acquired skill	1, 6, 7, 9, 12, 13
4, 5, 9, 10, 11, 12	peer modeling	1, 2, 3, 6, 7, 8, 13

NOTE: The counseling procedures are referred to by number as follows: 1) Williamson's procedure, 2) Ryan's reinforcement procedure, 3) Ryan's simulation procedure, 4) Healy's career counseling procedure, 5) The case study procedure, 6) EPS, 7) SIGI, 8) Roger's client-centered procedure, 9) Discovery group procedures, 10) Bates' time management procedure, 11) Sorenson's guided inquiry procedure, 12) Placement skill procedures, 13) Holland's SDS.

Emphasis on *systematic planning* distinguishes eleven of the procedures from the client centered and discovery counseling procedures. In both these procedures, a client is assisted in systematic planning, but he is not guided through a model of such planning as he is in the others.

Reinforcement is a prominent aspect of the Ryan, Healy, Bates, Sorenson, and placement procedures and in SIGI. Counselors employing those procedures selectively reinforce client behavior. Reinforcement may also be employed in the other procedures, but it is not directly prescribed.

Counselors following the client-centered and discovery methods encourage the client to recognize and discuss his feelings about himself. Although none of the procedures ignore the client's feelings about his developing self concept, only the discovery and client-centered procedures emphasize uncovering feelings to increase *self-acceptance.* In his procedure, Sorenson attends to a client's feelings to facilitate treatment, but he believes that it is counter productive for the client to dwell on his own negative feelings to develop self-acceptance. Rather, he emphasizes developing the skills whereby a client can realize his goal. When one achieves one's goal, suggests Sorenson, he increases his self-acceptance.

Utilization of Williamson's counseling, the Ryan procedures, the case conference procedure, EPS, and SIGI puts major emphasis on *integrating data* from tests, inventory scores, and grades into a client's planning. Clients are encouraged to select goals consistent with such information. Other procedures, particularly Healy's and Sorenson's, enable such data to be integrated, but they do not require it.

The specificity of problem and solution is a major concern of the counselor using the Williamson, Ryan, Healy, EPS time management, or guided inquiry counseling methods. In these procedures, clients must specify problems and/or plans in measurable terms before counseling proceeds. While specificity is desirable in all procedures, it is essential only to those noted.

Counselors utilizing all but the client-centered procedure must evaluate client progress on an ongoing basis in order to pace it. The client-centered counseling process has been evaluated most extensively, yet the counselor is not supposed to evaluate while counseling for fear he will become mechanical.

Transferability of the skills acquired in planning, goal setting, and self regulation is an intent of all the procedures, but Ryan's, Healy's, the case study, Roger's, Sorenson, and Bates' include components that encourage generalization of the planning and self-regulating skills developed. Thus, in the Ryan simulation and in the case study procedure, clients apply the principles of planning to several different cases; in the Healy procedure, clients label the steps of planning and problem solving and discuss plans and solutions in terms of the labels; in the Rogerian procedure, the counselor repeatedly models and rehearses the client in acceptance and deliberativeness; in his procedure Sorenson guides the client through uniform steps in analyzing different objectives and repeatedly labels what he has done; and in the Bates' procedure, clients also label what they have done in frequent summaries.

Peer modeling is appropriate in any of the procedures which can be used with groups. However, in the Healy, case study, discovery, Sorenson, Bates, and placement procedures clients are specifically encouraged to note and imitate desirable behavior of other clients.

LIMITATIONS

The thirteen procedures in this report have not been used extensively, and there is only limited research available to support their validity. This is an important limitation, but it can be corrected by counselors using and validating the procedures. However, there are other limitations including a limited number of problem-solving strategies, lack of provision for intervening on the client's behalf, minimal introduction to the role of agent which each of the procedures expects the client to play, lack of direct input by others involved in the client's career, and minimal efforts to assist the client who is trying to carry out his career plan. The latter limitations are discussed more fully below.

All procedures require a counselor to assist the client who is not benefiting from the learning program, i.e. to engage in problem-solving. A review of responses used in the different procedures, however, shows that there are few such techniques available. Particularly in group counseling, it would appear that there is need for specific sub-routines, perhaps individual sessions with the counselor, which would resolve various difficulties that clients have in keeping up with the counseling group.

Traditionally, counseling has focused on helping a person to marshall resources to achieve a goal. This has usually meant that the client is completely responsible for finding extracounseling resources. Today that attitude is changing. There is increasing acceptance of the propositions that some resources are not generally available unless the counselor intervenes directly and that such counselor intervention need not create a dependent client. None of the thirteen procedures described here, however, specifies interventions which a counselor might use to provide a client access to an extra-counseling resource. Although many counselors gain entry for clients to specific resources, such interventions are frequently not considered a part of counseling. They are regarded as another distinct service. However, two similar counseling cases could have radically different outcomes if one client were given access to resources, such as knowledgeable executives, volunteer work experience, etc., which the other was not. Likewise, two counselors might differ in their ability to secure access to external resources, particularly if they approached the task differently. Therefore, because some extra-counseling resources are not available unless a counselor intervenes and because replicability of counseling requires specification of any intervention, all thirteen procedures need to be extended by defining methods of interacting or consulting with resource persons. For example, in exploring his interests, a client may find that he has not had a certain experience which is part of a campus course that is not available to him at the time. Anticipating such a case, the counselor might incorporate in his procedure the action of contacting instructors to secure entry to parts of courses for selected students. To be replicable, the counselor should specify what students will be selected and how instructors will be contacted.

Clients are expected to become planners and problem solvers in all procedures, but only the client-centered, discovery, and guided inquiry procedures now have components which might be used for initiating the client into the role of agent. Many people believe and act as if their lives were determined by external forces (Rotter, 1966). For these people it will be difficult to assume the role of agent, and it is unlikely that they will be able to do so without a special inception phase. Likewise, many disadvantaged persons approach a middle-class counselor with suspicion and apprehension about his willingness to assist them in truly becoming agents of their lives (Kaple and Ullmer, 1973). This suggests that counselors need to develop special inceptions which will overcome that suspicion and apprehension.

All procedures, group or individual, approach career tasks as if they had meaning for only the client. No procedure provides for the involvement or the direct input of others (spouse, children, etc.) who are likely to be directly affected by the course of the client's career. Career counselors have not yet adopted ways to work either collectively or concomitantly with family members even though career planning could be more effective if a spouse's feelings and commitment to assist in a family member's career could be considered when formulating plans. Indeed, research on the careers of married women suggests that a wife's career success is dependent on her husband's reaction to her efforts. Increasing concern about careers by women suggest that a man no longer can expect his wife to accommodate herself to his arbitrary decisions. Consequently, the thirteen counseling procedures need to be extended to enable the direct input of the client's spouse or other family members.

There has been limited research on facilitating the execution phase of career development, although the client-centered, discovery, guided inquiry, time management, and placement skills procedures contain components which could help clients to make their jobs or educational programs more satisfying. Hoffnung and Mills (1970) have shown that group counseling improves success in on-the-job-training, and Slocum and Hand (1972) have indicated that human relations training facilitates development of supervisory skills. Such data and the availability of procedures certainly suggest such counseling could be productive. However, since teachers and work supervisors are directly involved in a client's training or work, counselors wishing to aid their clients as they implement plans should make provision to coordinate or collaborate with the teachers or supervisors who are involved. At present, counseling components for such cooperative efforts are not available, and consequently they need to be developed and validated.

In noting the intrinsic limitations of the procedures, it is hoped that counselors do not forget that currently the major concern is to validate the procedures—to apply them to junior college students and to determine how helpful they are in promoting vocational development. Consequently, this report concludes with a chapter on methods of assessing vocational development.

CHAPTER 5

METHODS OF EVALUATING CAREER DEVELOPMENT

THIS CHAPTER IS designed to help counselors use the thirteen procedures described in Chapters 2 and 3. Evaluation of the counseling process and measures of career development are discussed. Counselors must, to establish accountability, show that they are using specified procedures and periodically show that those procedures produce recognizable benefits. Thus, they must judge whether they counsel according to standard and whether their efforts lead to client gains. Unfortunately, there are few instruments for assessment of career development. Test constructors and counselors have only begun to recognize the need. Counselors, therefore, will frequently have to construct their own instruments for measuring the benefits of their counseling; it is unlikely that appropriate measures will exist for all a client's goals. Although the topic of constructing counseling outcome measures is beyond the scope of this report, the variety of measures described in this chapter can provide useful models for the counselor who would develop his own instruments.

EVALUATION OF THE COUNSELING PROCESS

Examination of the characteristics of a replicable counseling procedure indicates that to show that his counseling meets a standard, a counselor must verify that he has provided the correct exercises and responded appropriately to his client. Efforts to show replicability in counseling, however, typically have examined only the client-counselor interaction or counseling atmosphere (Marsden, 1971). Rogers and his students (1954, 1967) pioneered systematic evaluation of the counseling process, focusing on the counseling atmosphere because in client-centered counseling the counselor's major concern is that atmosphere. But even Rogers and his students acknowledged the need to assess more than the atmosphere to show that counseling was administered correctly. In some of their studies, Rogers and his colleagues (1967) assessed whether the client advanced through the phases of growth in addition to assessing atmosphere. Unfortunately, others assessing counseling, even counseling with a series of exercises, have ignored the need to verify that a client experienced each exercise.

Recognizing the need to evaluate the entire counseling process, Bates (1971) and Healy (1973) suggested approaches to the problem during development of career counseling procedures. Their approaches are different, but it is this author's judgment that either might be utilized to show that the procedures of his monograph are administered correctly. Consequently, both are described and contrasted here.

The approach being developed by the author and his students consists of dividing counseling into its components and rating whether each component is presented correctly. Consideration is also given to counselor's responses and their appropriateness. To evaluate the adherence of a counselor to Healy's procedure, for example, one would first check whether each component listed in Appendix F occurred. The counselor's responses within that component would, then be judged. Theoretically, client improvement should be a function of accurate presentation and appropriate counselor responses, but sufficient data are not yet available to test that hypothesis.

Bates (1971) defined her procedure by a script which prescribed each step of the counseling process, including counselor statements and responses for different client reactions. An excerpt of her script for the fourth session appears in Appendix H. Since the script is divided into distinct counselor statements, independent raters have only to judge whether counselor statements are the same or equivalent to the script statements to establish that counseling meets its criterion. In Bates' (1971) original study, her two raters agreed that the counselors performed according to script 95 percent of the time. Vivell's (1973) two raters judged that her three counselors adhered to the script at least 92 percent of the time.

Adequate research has not been done to establish which of the approaches has more utility. Both approaches provide for rating the occurrence of each counseling exercise and the effectiveness of the counselor in facilitating the operation of the exercise. Bates' approach requires only one rating while the author's approach requires two. Bates needs only one rating because she has specified her procedure in such detail that all appropriate counselor responses for an exercise are listed with each counselor's statement. Thus the counseling process can be judged in terms of whether each statement is correct rather than whether a component is present. This probably facilitates learning the procedure and insuring that every counseling idea has been presented. But by trying to account for all contingencies, the mature counselor is prevented from modifying or adapting an exercise to fit his client's unique needs. This may reduce the effectiveness of counseling. On the other hand, by prescribing only a general outline of the exercise by which a component is to achieve the client's subgoal, the Healy approach requires the counselor to constantly evaluate his client's progress to modify exercises by appropriate responses to the client. But because every thought element of an exercise is not specified, it should be more difficult to learn a counseling procedure and to insure that all counseling ideas are presented by specifying it according to the Healy approach. Since the thirteen procedures of this monograph can be specified by following either Bates or Healy, readers can try both approaches to determine which better meets their needs.

ASSESSING VOCATIONAL DEVELOPMENT

Counselors can validate career counseling procedures by assessing their clients' vocational development during counseling via pre-post or other appropriate quasi-experimental designs (Campbell and Stanley, 1963) and by supplementing those analyses with selected case studies (Thorenson, 1969). Most direct benefits of career counseling can be classified as information processing, planning, and execution. Information processing refers to obtaining, knowing, and accepting facts about one's self and existing opportunities, their requirements, and changing societal expectations. It is a lifetime task because every person needs to recognize and accept a changing identity shaped by his choices (Tyler, 1969) and changing social circumstances (Toffler, 1970). Planning refers to deliberating about and analyzing different alternatives in terms of assets, liabilities, values, goals, and obstacles to decide upon a problem-solving strategy. It is logical and essential if one assumes that he influences his career growth. Acceptance of responsibility for planning in adolescence is related to purposeful career activity in adulthood (Super, et al., 1969). Execution refers to carrying out plans: building skills, developing purposeful attitudes, securing and advancing in one's employment. The success of a client's execution is the ultimate criterion for judging the effectiveness of his information processing and planning. Several measurable criteria exist for each of the three general counseling goals. They are listed in Table V, while methods of measuring the criteria are discussed below.

TABLE V
CAREER COUNSELING CRITERIA

Information Factors	Contacts with information sources
Knowledge about information sources
Attitudes about obtaining information
Extent of career information
Accuracy of self-knowledge
Self-acceptance
Planning Factors	Knowledge about career planning
Extent of planning
Completeness of plans
Acceptance of responsibility for choice and planning
Realism of plans
Ability to solve career problems
Execution Factors	Attitude about career
Skills developed
Satisfaction with occupation
Satisfactoriness of occupational performance

Contacts with informational sources have been measured directly by counting the number of times a person does such things as borrowing reading material, visiting work sites, etc. and indirectly by asking the client to report the number of such contacts. Krumboltz (1963), Krumboltz and Thoresen (1964), Krumboltz and Shroeder (1965) have established that clients accurately report their information seeking behavior when they are asked about specific contacts (e.g., read the Occupational Outlook Handbook rather than read about jobs). Studies using such contacts as outcome criterion have shown that information seeking is increased by reinforcing expressed intent to obtain information, by exposing clients to live or taped models who seek information, and by various forms of non-replicable counseling. Researchers have composed their own lists of locally available information sources instead of using standardized lists.

Knowledge of informational resources refers to awareness of the people or aids giving assistance in career planning. Only two standardized scales of such knowledge are now available. Ryan (1968) developed ten open-ended questions and a scoring manual about information sources. Her scale has a two-week test-retest reliability of $r = .84$ (N=60) and, as noed in Chapter 2, it distinguished among students exposed to different kinds of counseling. Healy and Klein (1973) developed another ten item multiple choice scale about knowledge of informational sources, and it is now being validated.

Attitude about obtaining information refers to a person's expressed willingness to use specific resources in career planning. The Career Development Inventory (Super, et al., 1971) contains twenty-eight items asking the person whether he would utilize particular resources and whether the resource was helpful in the past. The scale has a test-retest reliability of .82 and a stability of .71 over one year.

Extent of occupational, educational and manpower information is an important factor in vocational development. In Super's Career Pattern Study (1957, 1960, 1969), ninth and twelfth graders' knowledge of occupational requirements, duties, work conditions, and demand clustered with other indices of vocational maturity and related to behavioral indices of such maturity at age twenty-five. In the Career Development Study, career information contributed to the Gribbons and Lohnes (1968) measure of vocational maturity in eighth, tenth and twelfth grades. Occupational information tests can also distinguish those students who receive career guidance from those who have not (Darcy, 1968; Super, *et al.*, 1971; Vriend, 1969).

Several tests and self reports of career information have been developed, although only limited data pertinent to their validity are available. The Career Development Inventory (CDI) (Super, *et al.*, 1971) includes a thirty item test of occupational information. Scores on the test correlated positively with the Readiness for Vocational Planning Scale (Gribbons and Lohnes, 1968), correlated with grade level, and increased after computer-assisted guidance. The CDI also contains eleven self-report items which assess one's knowledge of specific aspects of his preferred occupation. *The Woman's Career Information Test* (1970) contains sixty-five questions concerning occupational characteristics of special relevance to women such as "permits setting one's own hours."

The *Career Maturity Inventory* (Crites, 1973) contains two twenty item scales, one of which asks students to identify the name of a job from its description. The other asks one to identify the job which fits a set of personal characteristics. The *New Mexico Career Development Test* (Healy and Klein, 1973) contains both a twenty item scale of knowledge of appropriate work habits and a twenty-five item scale of knowledge about occupational characteristics.

Accuracy of self-knowledge or realism of self-concept has been widely studied as a goal for test interpretation and counseling (Myers, 1971; Tyler, 1969). It is usually assessed by comparing a person's self-report of a quality with an inventory score, a test score, or someone else's rating of the person. Sherwood (1966) found that specific descriptions of the quality to be rated increased agreement between the self-rating and test scores, while Mischel (1971) suggested that self-reports would be more accurate if the examiner specified the context in which the trait or quality would manifest itself. Accurate recall of test scores does not appear to depend upon whether the results are presented in groups or individually. Clients, however, feel more satisfied with individual reports (Folds and Gazda, 1966).

Accurate self-knowledge has not been found to be a major factor in vocational maturity until late adolescence (Super, 1972). In the Career Pattern Study, accuracy of self-knowledge in ninth grade did not relate to vocational maturity at age twenty-five, but twelfth grade scores for one of two samples did. Gribbons and Lohnes (1968) found that accuracy of self-knowledge in eighth, tenth and twelfth grade contributed to the Readiness for Vocational Planning Scale (RVP). Tiedeman and O'Hara (1959) found that although ability to accurately estimate interest, ability, and value scores increased throughout high school, accurate estimation of interests developed sooner than estimates of abilities or values. Similarly, Ginsberg, *et al.* (1951), hypothesized that aspects of self-knowledge develop differentially—knowledge of interests matures before knowledge of abilities, which matures before knowledge of values.

Self-acceptance or self-esteem refers to a person's regard for himself, to his judgment about the degree to which he is the person he wants to be. It has been measured by asking a person about his feelings about himself, by inventory (*Bills Index of Adjustment* (1951) and *Tennessee Self Concept Scale* (Fitts, 1964), by forced choice inventory (Ghiselli Self Esteem Scale, 1971), by comparing 'Q' sorts of self with 'Q' sorts of ideal self (Rogers and Diamond, 1954), and by comparing self-ratings with ideal self-ratings (Healy, 1973) and (Oppenheimer, 1966). Korman (1970), Super (1963), and Rogers (1951) hypothesized that esteem influences abiilty to integrate and use information and resources to make career decisions. Research suggests that high esteem persons choose compatible majors, occupations, and challenges more often than low esteem persons (Korman, 1970) and (Healy, 1973). Wiley (1961, 1969) has discussed the validity and reliability of many of the self-esteem measures, concluding that different measures were not equivalent. Consequently, she advised researchers to insure that their instruments reflect their stated definition of esteem. Generalizations about esteem thus become possible.

When it comes to planning factors, *Knowledge about career*

planning refers to one's awareness of the decisions and choice alternatives that exist in a career and to the methods for maximizing one's chances of achieving goals. Persons can manifest such ability by identifying and defining aspects of the planning process or by distinguishing effective from ineffective planning. So far only two standardized measures of this knowledge exist. The *Career Maturity Inventory* (Crites, 1973) and the *New Mexico Career Development Test* (Healy and Klein, 1973) contain twenty item scales which ask students to pick out the correct order of steps for reaching a goal.

Extent of planning refers to the amount of thought and number of resources utilized in making career plans. Several researchers have focused on this criterion. Super, *et al.* (1960, 1969) found that interview-derived scales of extent of planning clustered with other indices of vocational maturity and ninth and twelfth grade scores correlated significantly with behavioral indices of vocational maturity at age twenty-five. The Career Development Inventory (Super, *et al.*, 1971), includes fourteen items assessing extent of planning as part of the thirty-three item Planning Orientation scale. Hershenson (1966) constructed a twenty-three item inventory to assess the degree of thought given occupational choice. In support of its construct validity, he found that medical students made higher scores than college sophomores. Gribbons and Lohnes (1968) found that interview-derived measures of occupational and curricular planning contributed to the differentiation achieved by their RVP scale.

Completeness of plans refers to the number of factors relevant to a career that have been considered and for which there is provision. Although no measure of completeness of plans was located, one might examine whether a particular plan, described according to a standardized format contained specific goals, provided for accomplishing each step (school course, work experience, locating financial aid, etc.), listed contingency arrangements for unexpected events, and allowed on going evaluation of progress.

Acceptance of responsibility for choice and planning consists of concern about making choices and acknowledgement of personal responsibility for the planning of one's own career.

This construct has been assessed primarily by interview, although the new CDI contains eight items addressed to it as part of the thirty-three item Planning Orientation Scale. Super, *et al.* (1960) found that concern with choice and acceptance of responsibility for planning clustered with other indices of vocational maturity in ninth grade. Both ninth and twelfth grade scores correlated with indices of vocational maturity at age twenty-five. Gribbons and Lohnes (1968) found that similar interview-derived scores contributed to the differentiation obtained by the RVP scale.

Realism of plan refers to the feasibility of a person's executing the steps and accomplishing the objectives in a plan. It can be assessed by asking whether the steps of a plan logically relate to the objectives, and whether the person has the resources to accomplish the steps. For example, a community college freshman who plans to be an X-Ray technician in two years but works full time as a grocery clerk, and takes only general courses at night, does not have a realistic plan because the steps are not related to his objective. Likewise, a widower with three small children who plans to work and attend college full time for six years to become a lawyer has an unrealistic plan because it is unlikely that he will be able to fulfill the responsibilities of parent, employer, and student for so long a period.

To date, the realism of most career plans has been assessed by evaluating whether a person's talents, interests, and other resources are consistent with his occupational choice. Research has not shown that counselors judge the realism of their clients' plans accurately, but research does suggest that clients can judge the realism of their own plan. Hewer (1959, 1966) found that four counselors' judgments about the realism of the plans of eighty clients were not accurate seven years later. Her data also showed that 90 percent of the students had achieved their stated goals or similar ones within seven years. Her findings are encouraging if one regards the eighty plans as eighty realistic judgments. One group of judges then, the clients themselves, achieved 90 percent accuracy. From a review of the literature on the realism of college students' academic and vocational plans, Whitney (1970) also concluded that students were realistic in such planning. Unfortunately, research has not indicated the information which is needed to judge realism, but Hewer's and Whitney's (1970) findings indicate that it can be obtained by analyzing the manner in which students decide that their own plans are realistic.

Ability to solve career problems is the capacity to generate alternative solutions to career problems, to order the solutions in terms of their appropriateness, and to implement an appropriate solution. The *Career Maturity Inventory* (1973) contains two twenty item scales which assess the ability to both identify available alternatives and pick out the best solution to a career problem. The *New Mexico Career Development Test* (1973) assesses these aspects of problem solving with a ten item scale. Ability to solve career problems might also be assessed by asking clients to predict how well they would be able to deal with specific problems and about their experiences in solving typical problems, by asking others to rate the client's ability to solve career problems, or by testing a client's ability to generate solutions for hypothetical problems.

Under the execution category, *Attitude about career* refers to beliefs about one's ability to choose and to plan his career, to achieve satisfaction, to contribute to the common welfare, etc. Such attitudes are measured by asking a person to indicate whether he agrees with a statement or whether the statement is true of him. Several measures of attitude toward career, as opposed to attitude toward specific occupations, have been developed and four of them are described here.

The Career Development Attitude Scale is the most extensively used and researched career scale. Crites (1965, 1971) designed the scale to assess vocational maturity, which Super had defined as the degree to which a person has accomplished the vocational developmental tasks appropriate for his age. Crites' measure covers the domain of tasks referred to by Super (1963) as "crystallization, specification, and implementation." Scores on the scale have been found to increase with school grade and with exposure to vocational counseling. Although designed to measure five attitude factors, extensive analyses indicated that the scale is factorially complex; that is, items do not cluster into similar groups across different populations.

The *Vocational Decision-Making Check List* (Harren, 1972) is a fifty-six item inventory which taps attitudes about one's college major and occupation relevant to the developmental steps of exploration, crystallization, choice, and clarification described by Tiedman and O'Hara (1963). Initial studies of the inventory indicated that its scores discriminated among groups of college students who displayed different degrees of vocational maturity (Harren, 1966). Counselors at Southern Illinois University have found that the inventory is helpful in identifying vocational counseling goals for some students.

The *Women's Career Information Test* (1970) asks clients to register the degree of their agreement with seventy-five statements dealing with such topics as willingness to work after marriage, the need for challenge in a job, etc. The scale appears to measure five factors: desire for economic improvement, maintenance of traditional female role, opportunity to help and work with others, opportunity for challenge, and opportunity for job achievement.

The New Mexico Career Development Test contains a twenty-five item scale in which a client indicates his agreement with statements about the benefits of vocational training, the contribution of a worker to his community, the possibility of obtain- extrinsic and intrinsic satisfaction from working, and the interdependence of workers.

Career skills refer to abilities that are useful in obtaining and/or holding a job. These skills are assessed directly by observing a person do specific job tasks and by testing his knowledge of tools and job procedures. They are measured indirectly through supervisors' or instructors' ratings, by inference from the person's work and training history, and by self-report. Rehabilitation counselors have long provided supportive counseling to clients who were developing career skills. Counselors in educational instituitons can expect to do this in the future; recent emphasis on career education has made the development of such skills mandatory for every student.

Sorenson (in Bates, 1971) has proposed that there are two types of career skills—those required in a specific occupation and those required to function as a worker in any occupation.

Among the latter are communication, job seeking, and time management skills. Others have termed these general skills work habits (Shartle, 1959). Whatever the designation, these skills are assessed primarily by observing job performance in a standardized way or as part of supervision. Although industry and government have used aptitude testing extensively in employee selection, relatively few occupation-specific or general skills tests have been developed or are available outside the Armed Forces.

It is beyond the scope of this monograph to review the occupation specific tests, and tests of general career skills are now only beginning to be developed. Consequently, they cannot be discussed in a meaningful way. However, it is noteworthy that both the New Mexico Department of Education and the University of Houston Career Guidance Project (Meyer, 1971) are now testing measures of job seeking knowledge.

Satisfaction with occupation refers to the person's feelings about his work. It is a function of his present job and his frame of reference. Positive feelings are a sign of vocational maturity (Super, *et al.*, 1967) and a goal of career guidance. Occupational satisfaction has been studied extensively, with varied, often conflicting results. Crites (1969) has extensively reviewed the pertinent literature and the major measures of vocational satisfaction, and while his review will not be repeated here, those contemplating measuring vocational satisfaction will find his three observations especially noteworthy: vocational satisfaction is multidimensional, it is only slightly related to holding a position consistent with one's inventoried interests, and it is unclear whether vocational satisfaction causes or is caused by job performance.

Satisfactoriness of occupational performance indicates the level or quality of a person's job performance, but, unlike vocational or job success, its criteria can be established independently of the worker's feeling about his job performance. Job satisfactoriness is a major goal of career education and guidance, yet it is a relatively new concept introduced by Carlson, Dawis, England, and Lofquist (1963). Canonical correlations of satisfaction and performance scales indicated satisfactoriness is composed of two factors: performance (supervisor ranking, quality of work rating, promotability rating, recommendation for pay raise, and work adjustment rating) and conformance to rules (indices of lateness, accidents, and absences).

Many of the methods used to assess vocational success, including counting various forms of production, earnings, etc., are appropriate for assessing satisfactoriness. Those who would assess work satisfactoriness are referred to Crites' (1969) review of vocational success measures. As a consequence of that review, Crites recommended, in addition to traditional performance indices, assessments of success include measurement of the worker's maintenance of adequate interpersonal relations and his enthusiasm about learning new skills.

Conclusion

This report described replicable career counseling procedures which can be used in junior community colleges. Thirteen self-contained procedures were located by a survey of junior college counseling centers and by review of the professional literature. These procedures have been described in detail; their similarities, differences, and limitations have been noted; and methods for evaluating their benefits have been presented. The major focus of the report has been the replicability of the procedures because this common property enables the counselor to improve a procedure during and after use of it. This also helps him to justify allocation of time. The procedures were described in detail to facilitate their use rather than to suggest that counselors must follow them rigidly. Indeed, it is hoped that the descriptions presented here become both foundations, upon which more effective counseling are built, and stimuli, allowing counselors to detail and systematically study those procedures that are being devised. Furthermore, it is hoped that counselors will use the detailed descriptions in this monograph as models for describing their own procedures. With detailed descriptions of their procedures, counselors will be able to measure and to specify the benefits which accrue from each hour with an individual client or small group of clients. Such information will make it easier to show accountability for such contacts.

APPENDIX A

Plan of Career Counseling at Cabrillo College

Plan Otuline

Step 1. Fill out personal data questionnaire.

Step 2. Complete Strong Vocational Interest Blank ($1 fee) or A.C.T. Career Plan Profile ($6 fee).

Step 3. Write an autobiography.

Step 4. Complete Edwards Personal Preference Schedule (personality test).

Step 5. Complete the Study of Values.

Step 6. Complete aptitude testing and evaluation.

Step 7. Make preliminary estimate of career options.

Step 8. Complete an occupational survey.

Step 9. Make preliminary decision on an occupation.

Step 10. Create plan of action.

Step Details for Plan

Step 1. The personal data questionnaire includes family background, education, work experience, hobbies, and interests.

Step 2. The Strong Vocational Interest Blank measures interest in families of occupations, and the A.C.T. test measures general aptitude and vocational interest in job clusters.

Step 3. The autobiography is an account of the individual's life in terms of home and family relationships, interpersonal strengths and weaknesses, and personal hang-ups.

Step 4. The Edwards personality test measures fifteen normal personality traits.

Step 5. This involves a measurement of six value systems: economic, social, political, aesthetic, religious, theoretical.

Step 6. The Henmon-Nelson college aptitude test measures verbal and mathematical potential. The A.C.T. Career Planning Profile measures general aptitude in ten areas.

Step 7. Information from all measuring devices is synthesized, and career options are estimated.

Step 8. A particular occupation (student's choice) is surveyed.

Step 9. Career choice is made from a general occupational family.

Step 10. Decide training and educational program, including schools.

APPENDIX B

Excerpt from Reinforcement Counseling Group Session

The following typescript constitutes an excerpt of one small group counseling session in which the counselor used reinforcement counseling techniques. The group was made up of seven freshmen students enrolled in a community college. Six of the participants were male, and one was female. Four of the males were eighteen; one was seventeen, and one was nineteen years of age. The female participant was eighteen.

In this session the topic was "Personal Factors to Consider in Deciding on an Occupation." The main aims in this session were to have students identify various personal factors to be considered in choosing an occupation, determine sources for getting information on these personal factors, and consider ways of using personal data in making occupational decisions.

In the session counselor gave cues, leading questions to elicit responses from students relevant to the aims of the session. Counselor also gave verbal reinforcement, that is, showed encouragement and approval for responses of participants relating to the goals of the session.

Typescript

This is Instructor 3, Group 4, Topic 2. January 21, 1966.

Counselor: O.K. How's everybody today?

Student: Great.

Counselor: Today, we have a new member, Eugene. Is that right? Will you tell us something about yourself?

Gene: I went to High School in Washington, near Yakima. Graduated in 1965.

Appendix B

Counselor:	O.K. Do you know these fellow-students?
Gene:	No.
Counselor:	Well, this is Jerry, Chuck, Bruce, Dave, Larry, Gene and Leona. . . . (Leader indicates this is 2nd session and gives review of first session and project aims.) Now, did you figure out the topic for this session? The cue-initials of the three words are L A M.
Student:	Love and marriage.
Counselor:	The first two words are "looking at."
Student:	Looking at myself.
Counselor:	Right! The topic today is 'Looking at Myself." Last week you spent some time getting oriented just thinking about yourselves, why you were at Blue Mountain Community College, some of your problems and hopes. Today we want to talk about personal factors involved in choosing an occupation. In deciding on the kind of work one wants to do, what are some of the personal things to take into account?
Student:	Money. I mean how much money for example it will take for me to live on and be satisfied—do the things I want to do.
Counselor:	O.K. One personal factor to consider is the kind of life one wants to lead—the kind of things a person wants to do in order to be satisfied. Could you give an example?
Student:	Well, for example, a person might like to do a lot of hunting and fishing. Well, he should think about this and get into the kind of work that would let him take time off during hunting season and time for fishing.
Counselor:	This is a good example. This shows that a person needs to consider his interests—such as interest in outdoor activities, interest in sports—when con-

sidering different kinds of jobs. Do you have any other examples of taking into account one's interests? Bruce?

Student: Well take me for example. I like music. I am interested in music, so I met some guys who work in a radio station last summer. 'Cause I like music I got to hanging around the station with them, and then I got a chance to work as guest disc jockey at the station. And, I took it, and I was there three weeks checking records, taping. So, if I hadn't been interested in music, I wouldn't have been hanging around, and anyway I wouldn't have taken the job.

Counselor: That's a good example of how a person's interests can be considered in making a decision about whether to take a job or not. If you hadn't been interested in music, you probably would not have decided to take the summer job. Any other examples? Gene?

Gene: Well, I started out at about fifteen doing the thing that I wanted to do that interested me. My father works for Standard Oil, and I got to be around there a lot and got to know that I really was interested in that kind of work. My father got me a job with the company. I've been working with them ever since, and I hope to continue because I am doing what interests me. But if I didn't like cars and mechanics and that, I wouldn't have wanted to work there.

Counselor: Yes, that's a good example, too. Shows that even though someone else can be helpful in getting a job for you—it still is important to take into account your own interests in deciding whether to take the job or not. Like you, Gene, taking into account your interest in mechanical things. What about you, Dave?

Appendix B

Student: Well, I like people. People interest me. I'd like to work somehow so to work with people. I can't think of any example, don't have any idea what I want to do . . . but I guess I'll look for something to be around people.

Counselor: That's a good point. Just knowing that your interest in people will be important to consider in looking at different jobs is important. Chuck, what about you?

Student: I can give you an example of what not to do. I had a job in a dental lab. Might of been interesting . . . but I don't know. I didn't like it. I just took the job. Wanted to make some dough.

Counselor: You feel that you didn't consider your interests when you took the job?

Student: Yah. I just went to work. I made false teeth. And the dentist got the money. Of course, he has lots more education. The lab charges fifty-five or sixty dollars and the dentist charges about two hundred and fifty to the person. I worked in The Dalles, but I didn't like it.

Counselor: How do you think you could have avoided getting into a job that you didn't particularly like by taking into account your interests?

Student: I don't know. I didn't know I didn't like it till I got there.

Counselor: Bruce, any ideas about this?

Student: You could have found out first what did interest you and then you have to see if the job gives you what you want. Like me. I like music. So working as disc jockey was O.K. Or, say, like Dave, he likes to work with people—and he knows this—and so working to make false teeth wouldn't do anything for him 'cause there's a lot of difference between being where there's people and where there's just false teeth. (Laughter)

Counselor: Fine. Fine. That's a good example, Bruce. Shows how a person needs to find out about his interests first, and then consider if the job will be one that will let him satisfy his own interests.
And, how do you think personality characteristics influence your choice of jobs?

Bruce: Have to like the people around you.

Student: That's not true, you don't have to.

Bruce: You don't have to be buddy buddy, but if you are going to work with people you should like to be around them.

Counselor: What do you mean by that, Bruce?

Bruce: If I had to work side by side with someone I can't stand, I just couldn't take it.

Counselor: Some jobs require working with hands, some with ideas, some with things, some with people. . . . Would this be a factor to consider in making a choice?

Bruce: Sure, if you're not able to work with people you're in trouble.

Counselor: You feel getting along with others is important. Gene, what do you think?

Gene: The ability to get along with people would mean a lot in a job when you are meeting the public.

Counselor: All right, then you need to consider whether you like working with people, in choosing a job. What else?

Student: I think you have to think about security. I mean a lot of people just have to have security. Others . . . well they just don't feel that way. They don't care if they are out of work for a while. Guess some guys seem to like to get that unemployment every so often. Now others, they just want a check every month. Some jobs don't go year round.

Appendix B

Counselor: Yes, that's a good point. A person needs to think about how important having security is to him, and then think about the kinds of jobs where he would get the degree of security he wants. Good point. What else? What other personal factors can you think of?

Student: Well I think you got to think of how important is it to have advancement. I mean some guys don't care if they ever amount to anything. I mean they don't care if they get a better job or I guess even if they get more money. But other guys—well, they are gung-ho for moving up. They want to get a better job all the time. So you've got to think about this. If you want to advance—then you've got to get in a job where you can advance.

Counselor: Yes, taking into account one's need for advancement is important. What about intelligence, or lack of it? Does this have anything to do with choosing a job?

Student: That depends upon the field.

Counselor: It does depend upon the field. Good point. Does education play a major role in choosing a job, Dave?

Dave: One must have capabilities for any job. Depending upon the company, you must learn to do a job in a particular way. But you have to have the capabilities.

Counselor: Yes, what about intelligence, Dave, mental ability?

Student: Intelligence, you have to have some mental ability to succeed.

Counselor: O.K. You have to have some degree of intelligence to get started.

Student: One of my friends told us about a guy who dropped out of school at eighteen and eventually became head of a large company.

Student: Well, that is unusual and not the rule.

Bruce: Of course, but it can happen. The point is that it takes more than intelligence and education to guarantee success.

Counselor: What part does intelligence play in deciding on the kind of work one wants to do? Do some jobs require more intelligence than others?

Student: They all need ability, but some require more intelligence.

Counselor: Yes, I think this is the main point here. Good idea. How about physical health?

Student: It depends upon the demands of the job, they differ.

Counselor: It depends upon the demands of the job. Can you give us an example.

Student: Take a doctor . . . makes his rounds in hospital . . . office hours . . . house calls. That's hard on him, and if he's sick a lot he loses patients.

Student: Who wants to go to a sick doctor. (Laughter)

Student: That's just the point.

Counselor: Good point . . . physical condition. In choosing a job you need to consider the physical demands. Any other examples.

Student: One with a bad back shouldn't try to do heavy construction, nor should one with a bad leg try to do a job that requires lots of walking.

Counselor: Good examples. Can you see a person not being hired because of a certain physical handicap?

Student: Sure . . . that would be a let down, but he would have to adopt (sic) to it. I guess lots of jobs have physical requirements before you can be hired.

Appendix B

Counselor: Right! True. And, one must consider these factors in choosing. These are good points to consider—one's mental ability and physical strength and characteristics.

Student: Yes, if he were in a job and developed an allergy or something, he would either have to adjust or change jobs.

Counselor: Yes, these are good ideas. Good points. Leona, what are your feelings?

Leona: I agree with what they have said.

Counselor: Gene, can you add anything? Can you think of any other personal factors to consider? What about special aptitudes? How about those in thinking about the kind of job one wants.

Gene: Either have them or you don't. Special interests can be developed.

Counselor: Interests can be developed. O.K. Do some jobs require more than one aptitude?

Student: Yes.

Counselor: Can you give an example?

Student: Take radio . . . you have to have a good English background.

Student: I disagree . . . have you ever listened to radio?

Counselor: What about aptitudes?

Student: Newsmen on radio, like a reporter on the scene, must get along with people and must know how to talk.

Counselor: O.K. Anyone else give an example where more than one aptitude is involved. Dave?

Dave: Huntley and Brinkley for example . . . they have to have background in history . . . and be intelligent. Must have good English background and know how to read.

Counselor: Uh huh . . . good point. Gene, what special aptitudes are required in work at the service station?

Gene: At Standard service stations you need knowledge of engineering and be able to get along with people and if one is to advance very far he must have ability to sell.

Counselor: Good points. You've described quite a few special aptitudes to consider. I can see you aren't finished with this yet, but our time is up for this session, so we'll have to quit. During the week, how about seeing just how many of the points we talked about—the personal factors you mentioned and we discussed in considering different jobs—how about seeing how many of these you can relate to yourselves. For example, just what are your interests? Then, next week, when we start we'll take a few minutes to talk about these.

Now, before we break up today, how about a quick summary of this session. What were the main points today? Bruce?

Bruce: We talked about the personal things to consider in deciding what kind of work to choose. Deciding upon what one goes into. We decided you need to know about these things, and that it will require certain degrees of aptitudes, intelligence, training, liking to be with people . . .

Dave: . . . and personality traits . . . and . . .

Counselor: Good! Chuck, what is another very important factor we discussed?

Chuck: Health.

Counselor: Yes, these are all important. And we agreed they should be considered. O.K. We accomplished quite a bit in this discussion today. You brought out a number of good points. Sorry we can't continue now, but next week we are going to be talking about how we fit into the world of work, same time, same station! See you here then. In the meantime—be giving some thought to your own personal characteristics. So long.

APPENDIX C

Student Profile

DECISION PROJECT
BLUE MOUNTAIN COMMUNITY COLLEGE—
PENDLETON, OREGON

E-13   URIA FOX

Uria Fox is eighteen years old. He is 5 ft. 11 in. tall and weighs 195 lbs. He is in excellent physical condition. Uria graduated from high school in June and has been working at home during the summer with his step-father. He lives with his parents and half-sister about ten miles out of town on a small farm, and his half-sister is in the first grade. Uria's mother was born on an Indian reservation. His father died when he was eight years old, and his mother remarried when he was ten. He and his mother then went to live on his step-father's farm. Uria's mother never has worked outside the home.

Uria's hobbies are sports, bulldogging and horses. He was on the football team in high school and made name for himself. He doesn't know what he wants to do now.

Name: URIA FOX

Kuder Vocational Percentile		*Kuder Personal* Percentile	
40	Outdoor	86	Group Activity
5	Mechanical	66	Stable Situations
33	Computational	15	Dealing with Ideas
85	Scientific	13	Avoiding Conflict
76	Persuasive	79	Directing Others
22	Artistic		
15	Literary		*Edwards Preference Schedule*
30	Musical		Percentile
68	Social Service	20	Achievement
63	Clerical	18	Deference
		65	Order
	General Aptitude Test Battery Percentile	95	Exhibition
		12	Autonomy
48	General Learning Ability	76	Affiliation
46	Verbal Aptitude	27	Intraception

APPENDIX C (Cont.)

General Aptitude Test Battery
Percentile (Cont.)

39 Numerical Aptitude
78 Spatial Aptitude
68 Form Perception
70 Clerical Perception
84 Motor Coordination
28 Finger Dexterity
88 Manual Dexterity

American College Test
Percentile

2 English Usage
14 Mathematics Usage
10 Social Science Reading
9 Natural Science Reading
4 Composite

My Vocational Choice

1. College
2. ....
3. ....
4. ....
5. ....

Edwards Preference Schedule
Percentile (Cont.)

60 Succorance
70 Dominance
40 Abasement
22 Nurturance
10 Change
58 Endurance
79 Heterosexuality
68 Aggression

Otis Quick Scoring Mental Ability
104

Average High School Grades

D English, 4 yrs.
C History, 2 yrs.
B Mathematics, 1 yr.
C Science, 2 yrs.
D Typing
  Bookkeeping
  Shorthand
C Music, Art ½ yr.
B Wood, Metal
B Plastics, 3 yrs.
  For. Lang.
C Auto. Mech., ½ yr.
A P.E., 4 yrs.
B Agric., 2 yrs.
C Health Occ., 1 yr.
  Home Ec.
  Dis. Ed./Div. Occ.

Typescript of Counseling Session Using Simulation Materials and Counselor Reinforcement

The following typescript constitutes a transcription of one small group counseling session in which simulation materials and reinforcement counseling techniques were used. Typescript begins at conclusion of opening interval. The group was made up of seven participants, all of whom were enrolled as freshmen in a community college. Five of the group members were male and two were female. Four of the male members were eighteen and one was nineteen years of age. Both female members were eighteen. In this session, students were given a chance to simulate decision-making by a student similar to themselves in background and individual characteristics. Primary aims in this session were for students to learn to use information in identifying alternatives and to consider consequences of the different alternatives in making decisions.

Typescript

Session 1 A SRC (Uria)

Counselor: Now that we have become acquainted with one another, let's begin our task for today. Remember in our meeting on Monday we talked about the small group sessions we would have each week, where we would plan the lives of fellows and girls much like the students here at Blue Mountain. Remember we agreed that the main purpose of these sessions would be to help you become better able to make your own decisions about your work career and educational plans. Your goal, then, is to become better equipped to make educational and work plans for yourselves. During the rest of this quarter in our small sessions we will make educational and occupational plans for four students—with backgrounds much like yours. For each person we will have information about his background. As you plan his or her life you can ask me for additional information, or you may wish to seek information elsewhere. For each person I'll tell you about a few unplanned events —things that happen that the person hasn't counted on and which may call for changing plans.

All right, now, I want you to meet Uria. Uria is a fellow much like yourselves. Here is a data sheet about his family, his school record in high school, his interests, abilities and aptitudes. You can see that Uria lives just out of Pendleton with his mother and step father and half sister on a small farm. They don't have too much money, but they have been able to make a living—from the farm. Uria's mother and step father both dropped out of school. Uria's grandparents lived on the reservation (Indian). Uria's half sister is in first grade. Here are the scores from the tests Uria took last

Appendix C 101

spring in high school. You can see that his highest interest scores on the Kuder were in scientific and persuasive. He also had above average aptitude in spatial and motor on the General Aptitude Test that the Employment Office gave last May. He does not seem to like things to change . . . seems to enjoy security; likes things to remain stable . . . likes to feel secure. He seems to like being with people. Here is his high school record. You can see he was outstanding in athletics—had A in physical education all through high school. His other grades are C's and D's.

Here is the personal inventory sheet he completed last spring. He states that his occupational goal is "college." He also said that his hobbies are bulldogging, horses, and sports.

Now you will want to use this information in making plans and decisions for Uria. You are to put yourselves in Uria's place and together you are to make decisions and plans concerning his education and work for the four or five years right after his graduation from high school. Uria will need to decide what school he will attend after high school, if any; what he will take in school, if he goes; what additional information he will look for; what activities he will try out before deciding on a full-time job—which will be the beginning of his work career.

In making these decisions for Uria you will want to think about different possibilities and the consequences of taking different actions. Your goals today are to learn to use information in identifying alternatives; and to consider consequences before making decisions.

All right, now you have Uria's background. Remember he is just finishing up the summer's work on the farm. He finished high school last June. His first decision is what is he going to do this fall. Will he go on to school? What do you think?

Rick: I think he should go to work on the farm. I mean that's it. He ...

Counselor: What information do you think he will want to consider to help him decide about going to school this fall, Elaine?

Elaine: He seems to like mathematics. He should look at that. He has B in high school math.

Counselor: Yes, his high school record is important to consider in thinking about whether to go to school or not. What else?

Randy: Well on this he scored high in clerical. And on this he was high in persuasive too.

Counselor: Good points to notice. What might this information mean to Uria in thinking about whether to go on to school or not?

Elaine: He probably would enjoy working in some kind of clerking. He didn't like change. Clerking is just a lot of the same thing. Maybe he would like to be a clerk.

Counselor: These are good observations and very important considerations. Does it seem then that clerical work might be one possibility for Uria? Are there other points he should consider? How does this relate to his problem about deciding whether or not to go to school this fall?

Steve: Well, he is just average in intelligence. Look at his high school grades and his IQ. I don't care what he wants to do. He's got to think about how smart he is.

Counselor: Yes. These are good points to think about. How will these factors—his mental ability, his school records, his achievement in school so far—affect his decisions? What about his thinking of clerical work as a possible job choice? How would this affect his going on to school?

Appendix C

Steve: I don't know that it will keep him from doing clerking. That doesn't take too high an IQ. That speaker yesterday said that much. He should stay away from college though—from any kind of that 'cause hes just not that good. Even though he says he likes school O.K., he's no hot shot student and probably he'd flunk out at U of O. I know a guy like him and he did flunk out. Now he's a mess.

Rick: Ya, but he said he wanted to go to college. Look the only thing he wrote for choice was college. He still wants to go to college, and . . .

Clara: Yes, this is what he wrote, but he wasn't thinking about all that might happen . He probably wrote that last year when we filled out all that stuff. Remember?

Counselor: Yes. This information is from the forms completed while he was in high school last year. Now, the question is what does he decide, now that it is getting to the end of the summer, taking into account the information he has about himself and what he knows about different kinds of work. Will he want to go on to school this fall? Art?

Art: Well, he has worked out on the farm a lot; and he knows about that, but he likes people, and he's high on social service . . .

Rick: Why doesn't he just stay on the farm. He should stay on the farm. That's just it.

Counselor: The facts that he enjoys working with people and is high on social service are important points to consider. Are there other things—other information to take into account?

Art: Well he like sports—football, bulldogging, horses.

Rick: He should think about farming.

Counselor:	So, does it seem that thinking about farming—something related to farming—might be a possibility to consider, along with other possibilities?
Art:	Ya.
Counselor:	Of course, he might come up with other possibilities later, don't you think; even though right now he might want to make his decision about whether or not to go to school this fall, taking these two possibilities, clerical and farming, into consideration. What do you think?
Steve:	Well, he could decide whether to go to school or not. He hasn't got all day. If it's already the end of summer.
Counselor:	This is an important point. He really does need to make some kind of decision right away about school, doesn't he? What do you think?
Randy:	One thing, farming is something he knows. He's had work on the farm, and he knows it.
Counselor:	Good point to consider—his experience on the farm, so he has information about the kinds of work involved and can use this information as he considers alternatives.
Rick:	It's a normal thing to do to go on with the farm. I know a lot of guys around here who just naturally take over when their dad gets old. They just stay. Don't even go to school.
Counselor:	What other information might he consider in thinking of farming. Are there different kinds of agriculture—related jobs that he might want to investigate? Clara?
Clara:	His outdoor score was not high.
Counselor:	This is something to be considered, isn't . . .

Al: Yes, but he likes sports though, and baseball and football. He likes horses and bulldogging and that sure as hell is outdoors. I don't think you can go altogether on what these tests say. Sometimes they are all off.

Counselor: Good point. You think it takes more than just looking at test scores to make decisions? Are you suggesting that Uria might want to look at all the test information and also think about other things he knows about himself—things he enjoys doing; things he does well; the kinds of situations he enjoys? In looking at all these things, what does it seem Uria might want to do this fall?

Al: Well, he likes sports and baseball. He likes horses and bulldogging. He might like the farm O.K.

Counselor: Are you suggesting that one possibiilty for Uria would be agriculture-related work?

Al: Ya, that's one thing for sure.

Counselor: Would you say then, that at this point Uria might want to consider agriculture-related jobs and clerical work as two possibilities?

All: Ya. Yes.

Counselor: What do you think would be the consequences for Uria if he should go into either of these kinds of work?

Al: I agree with what Art said. Farming is something he knows more about. He likes working the horses and bulldogging. He's not sure about clerking—what it really means. He might not like it. And with farming he's got a good idea and with clerking it's anybody's guess.

Counselor: These seem important considerations. What do you think he might want to decide now. Remem-

	ber, it is almost time for fall term, so if he is going to go on to school he will need to make some immediate decisions. What do you think?
Steve:	Looks like the thing to decide now is to do something with farming. He can find out more about these other jobs too. He might want to work at something for a company or the government, and then when his dad gets old he'd take over.
All:	Ya. Yes.
Art:	But I say he wants to go to college and two years of college won't hurt him. He can get a better idea of what he wants to do.
Counselor:	Steve, what information will Uria need to consider in thinking about whether to go on for more schooling this fall?
Steve:	Well, he's got to figure out if he needs to go to school, to college, to get into the kind of work he wants. He could . . .
Counselor:	All right. Good point. Then, if he has tentatively decided on clerical work—some kind of job in this field—or farming—some kind of agriculture-related work—the question is does he need to go school this fall?
Randy:	If he goes to school for two years before he starts full time work, maybe he can even learn enough to do something with it, the farm, make more out of it. His old man never made money. Maybe he can make something there.
All:	Sure. Yes.
Counselor:	Taking these factors into consideration, do you say that Uria will want to enroll in school for this fall—go to school for two years?
All:	Yes. Ya.

Appendix C

Counselor: Then, where will he go to school? Which school will he go to?

Steve: We already talked about that. He can't make it at U of O. He'll flunk out. Be a mess. We decided he would go to a community college. Like here. He doesn't need a degree to be a farmer or a clerk, and like I said you can find out a lot more about other jobs here too.

All: Yah. He goes here.

Counselor: That's fine. It looks as if Uria has considered consequences of taking a four-year college as opposed to community college, and in terms of his background in school and his decision to look into the general occupational areas including agriculture-related and clerical—he has decided to go to community college. Fine. Now, I have some information about Uria that you will want to take into account. Just before the term begins, an unexpected event happened. Uria's father is in an accident and has to go to the hospital. He will be there for several weeks. How will this influence Uria's decision about going to school this fall?

Al: Maybe he could stay out of school fall term. This would give him time to work on the farm. This way he could get the feel of running it. See if he likes it.

Counselor: Sounds like a possibility. What about this?

Rick: Probably with the added responsibility of taking over the running of the thing like his father did,, he probably would . . . well it'd be different from just working like he is now. He could see if he likes it.

Counselor: You think having responsibility of running the farm would give him more of a chance to see if he likes it?

108 *Career Counseling in the Community College*

All: Hey. This would be a good deal. He could use his math too. He'll have a lot of figuring to do. My old man always is.

Counselor: So one consequence of his planning to stay out of college and to take over at the ranch this fall would be that it would give him a chance to see how he likes the managing part of farming. Right? And it would give him a chance to see how he could use his math background, too? Any other consequences?

Art: Ya, I think this is going to louse things up. If he stays out of school fall term, it would be easier to stay out another term and another and maybe never go to school.

Counselor: You mean one consequence of staying out would be he might never get started to school? Clara?

Clara: Well, it might come to be a habit and he'd never get started.

Counselor: Very possible. So this is one possible consequence of his staying out of school this fall and just taking over on the farm while his father is sick. What else might he do?

Al: There's something else about his staying out, the draft will get him. I think he should go to school.

All: Ya.

Steve: He can go to school and fix his schedule to get home early. That way he can still get some hours work in on the farm. He'll have to plan his schedule.

Counselor: So this is another possibility—going to school but getting a schedule to get home early. What would be the consequences of this action?

Randy:	Well, it would be O.K. He could get in the courses and still keep the farm going.
Counselor:	All right. Then, does it seem that after thinking of the consequences of staying out of school as compared to going to school this fall, that Uria will decide on going with a light schedule? Is this right, Rick?
Rick:	Yes, but he has to schedule his courses so he can get home early to work on the farm.
Art:	He is going here instead of U of O and that will make it easier for . . .
Steve:	Ya. This is what he does.
Counselor:	All right. Now, then, what about the courses?
Rick:	He can ask the counselor to do the schedule.
Counselor:	Elaine, what do you think? What does he need to consider in deciding on his schedule for the fall?
Elaine:	He can be taking things that have to do with farming. If he's going to be a better farmer than his father. And, he can find out more about other jobs, too.
Counselor:	All right. Good. Now what do you think he might want to take? Here is the schedule of courses for the fall, and the catalog of all the courses here. Maybe these will have some information to help Uria decide. (They study bulletins.)
Randy:	Look at this. This technical agriculture thing. I'd take this. Says for training for business, mechanical, producing parts of business. That's . . .
Steve:	Yah. That's a good idea. He gets math . . . like that and animal science. He'll like that. He likes

	horses and all. I don't know how he'll go for this plant science. That could be a dud. Will he like engines (combustion)? Was there something on . . . Yah, but he isn't going to like this . . . communication?
Clara:	Yes, but he doesn't have to take that, not till later.
Al:	Besides he has to get home early remember, and English . . . What about this? Industry practices? What's that about?
Steve:	Maybe he can get ideas of other jobs like business parts of farming. But let's leave this out now. He can take these others, math Monday, Wednesday, Friday, 9; plant science Tuesday, Thursday 9 to 10:30; animal science Monday, Wednesday, Friday at 11. When is the engines one?
Clara:	It's on Monday, Wednesday and Friday at 1:00. He can't take that.
Rick:	Yes he can. He can leave at 2 and be home by 3 at the latest and that gives him time. Besides if he doesn't take it now he'll be loused up for next time. I know, that happened to me in high school.
Counselor:	Good point, Rick. Good points that you have considered in looking at alternatives for Uria's schedule. It's especially good to look at the prerequisites as you did. As you pointed out, Rick, if Uria doesn't get the course in combustion engines this fall, he won't be able to take the second part of the course which is offered only in the winter. Now then how many hours does Uria sign up for?
Clara:	He has twelve hours, I think.
Rick:	Yah, twelve hours.
Steve:	Yeh, that's it. That's all he can take and run the farm.

Appendix C 111

Counselor: All right, now. I have some information about Uria for you to consider. The fall quarter gets underway. Uria takes the courses related to agricultural technology and keeps the farm going while his father is sick. In November his father is ready to take over again. What will this mean to Uria? What about winter term?

Randy: Well, that will depend on his grades. What grades did he get?

Counselor: Good point to consider. According to information on Uria, his grades for fall term are all C's.

Steve: Well. He only had twelve hours and nothing that he couldn't understand.

Art: Yes. That's right.

Randy: Then why not just go ahead and take the next terms courses like they are here in the book. He could take the full course this time 'cause he won't be working.

Counselor: That sounds like a possibility. What do you think? Steve, you mentioned that Uria might get information about other jobs. What about this?

Steve: Well, he could find out about different kinds of jobs . . . like something that might let him be with people. . . .

Art: Say, what about this police course? Look at this. He likes people and he's big enough, and this might be a possibility, and . . .

All: Ya. Yah.

Counselor: Yes, this sounds like a good idea. Now, do you have any idea where he might get that kind of information—in addition to what he will learn from his classes and the catalog that you have here?

Steve: Well, I know Mr. Heyer said there were books in his office that had information about different kinds of jobs, and we could use them anytime, and I think there is a book in the library on this.

Counselor: These sound like good sources for getting added information about occupations. Do you think it might also be a good idea to talk to . . .

Steve: Yah, my high school teacher. He'd know a lot about this.

Counselor: Good. I hate to break in here, but I see our time is up for today. It looks as if Uria is off to a good start, despite a couple of problems that came up for him. The next time you can plan Uria's life for the next couple of years. Before we stop today, how about summarizing what happened in our session today? Rick?

Rick: Well, the main things that happened. We decided to start out with farming. We thought about being a clerk, but it didn't seem too good for him. Farming was more like what he knew, let him be out-of-doors, and he could find out about different kinds of jobs that have to do with farming, and business and clerical and police work . . . those others that were in the catalog, and he can look into these. I got the idea myself of having to think about all that might happen to a guy in deciding on something. I never thought about coming here before or, you know, not coming. I just came but I didn't really know what I was here for, I guess. I never thought about all this.

Counselor: Good observation, Rick. I agree, it is important to think of consequences of different actions in making plans for work and schooling. Anything else to add? Elaine?

Elaine:	Well, he decided against a university. He didn't need it . . . He
Art:	He . . .
Steve:	He didn't need university . . . being a farmer or a policeman . . . he didn't need it. So that's why he went here. I got the idea that you know you got to think about all this stuff, like how smart you are and what you're going to do and that stuff, and not just say "college" like he did on that test.
Randy:	Yes, and I got an idea on taking courses, like he decided at first on the ag tech course. It was closest to farming, and he could get more ideas on other jobs that he might want to do. That's a lot like me. I'm going to look up that stuff in the books we talked about, for me.
Counselor:	Very good. Al, anything to add?
Al:	Well, he thought about it, and he looked at the college catalog. He thought about it because he wanted to take something to do with farming, I guess, and didn't know what to take, but . . .
Steve:	That's right. He talked about it and decided on taking something that had to do with farming at first, and looking at the college catalog, that gave me an idea about using the catalogs.
Counselor:	Good. Anything else?
Rick:	You got to think what happens if you do things, like if he stayed out completely he never would go back.
Counselor:	That's fine. A good point to mention. You've done a good job of summarizing our session today, and you've done a fine job of pointing up the importance of using information to decide on alternatives. You've pointed to the need to think of conse-

quences before taking steps, too. Very good. Next time we will complete Uria's plans to the time he goes into work full time. In the meantime, you might want to be looking up some of the information you mentioned he will be needing to make up his mind about his future educational plans and work decisions.

And, how about during the coming week, looking up information on law enforcement for Uria, and seeing if you can do some of the same things for yourselves that you have done for Uria today—look at your own interests and aptitudes and see what kinds of work might be possibilities for you to consider . . . look in the references in the occupational library to see what kinds of jobs are listed that might be possibilities for you . . . talk to people about different kinds of jobs . . . O.K.? Bye, now. See you next week.

APPENDIX D

Personal Traits

withstand pressure

careful and neat
dignified

stick-to-itiveness
bears hardship to obtain goals
ambitious
easily accepts rules

self-reliant

unconventional
honest
likes being with people
sympathetic
believes in strict rules
likes variety in a job
likes taking risks
accurate and precise
always examines own motives
has sense of humor
concerned for others

needs "yes" and "no" answers
has to feel free

helps others
likes clerical jobs
turned on by math

interested in science
learns math easily

does clerical jobs quickly
decisive
expresses himself well
imaginative

looks at ideas from all angles
likes mental challenges
solves problems systematically
digs art
has to keep active

has large vocabulary
good at simple tasks

tuned into what's happening
confident
carefree
thinks before acting
accepts criticism well
patient
cheerful
relaxed
emotionally stable
poised

outgoing
works best by himself

organizes socials well

without perjudice

friendly and cheerful
good muscle coordination
good manual dexterity

good memory
easily uses old knowledge in new situations
family man (woman)

likes children
mature about sex
writes well

learns quickly

quick-fingered
quick-reflexes

a leader
go-getter

enjoys recreation
likes cultural and community activities
daydreamer

digs business
mechanical inclined
likes outdoors
religious
interested in flying
artistic
patriotic
has to be admired
easily identifies things from their blueprints
tall
easily sees slight differences in colors
strong

can detect small differences in sound frequency
good sense of balance
wants quick social change
can detect small difference in loudness of sound
physically attractive
has expensive tastes

values money

lives by schedule
alert

APPENDIX E

Holland's Six Occupational Clusters

1
accountant
business machine
  operator
cashier
legal stenographer
credit manager
airline ticket clerk
telephone operator
bank teller
secretary
business teacher
keypunch operator
civil service clerk

2
actor
artist
architect
drama coach
editor
entertainer
advertising man
designer
interpreter
interior decorator
journalist
fashion model
writer

3
administrative asst.
airline stewardess
banker
buyer
economist
truck dispatcher
sales engineer
contractor
governmental official
production manager
supermarket manager
attorney
radio announcer
salesman
real estate salesman
bank executive

4
recreation administrator
athlete
bartender
social worker
cosmetologist
counselor
insurance correspondent
dental hygienist
dietician
librarian
historian
home economist
interviewer
nurse
physical therapist
politician
retail saleswoman
school principal

5
baker
shoemaker
bookbinder
bricklayer
carpenter
typesetter
cook
civil engineer
draftsman
fireman
forester
machinist
sailor
plumber
auto mechanic

6
airplane pilot
anthropologist
biologist
chemist
physician
dentist
engineer aid
mathematician
research analyst
TV repairman
psychologist
oceanographer
X-ray technician
laboratory technician
tool and die maker
computer programmer

APPENDIX F

Components of Group Career Counseling

Session	Components
1	Introduction and explanation of client role Presentation of clients and their concerns Overview of procedure Relation of process to client concerns Selection of work-relevant qualities Sharing important qualities Summary/future agenda
2	Identification of client concerns Report of extracounseling tasks Explanation and selection of 'representative occupations' Sharing representative occupations Description and illustration of rating Discovery of methods for occupational exploration Occupational rating Deciding on needed occupational information Summary/future agenda
3	Reports of explorations of occupation Summary of previous sessions Discussion of self-ratings Discovery of methods of self-appraisal Self-rating Selection of self-characteristics for exploration Computation of difference scores Reaction to difference scores Summary of session/future agenda
4	Reports of extracounseling exploration Summary of previous sessions Further reactions to difference scores Planning based upon difference scores Clarification of dissatisfaction with difference scores Summary of session/future agenda
5	Report of extracounseling activities Summary of previous sessions Additional client plans Selection of possible obstacles to plans Problem solving Summary/close

Excerpts of Selected Components

SESSION 1: **OBTAINING COMMITMENT AFTER EXPLANATION OF PROCEDURE**

Counselor: Tell us Barbara, in what way will you be helped by attending these meetings?

Barbara: Well, you said we would consider what we want to do and find out what jobs allow that. I need to do that because I am not sure about what I want to do, and I'd like to see how the others do it. Did you say we would take tests?

Counselor: Like Fran, you feel a need to think through what you want to get from working and see what jobs might have those things. Good! We'll be doing that. And testing, we won't give you tests here, but you can see Mr. C in the Counseling Center for testing if you feel testing will provide needed information. Does counseling seem like it will help you Barbara?

Barbara: Yeah, it sounds O.K.

SESSION 1: **SHARING QUALITIES**

Paul: Some of the qualities important to me are high salary, entertaining, big business, be my own boss, and having recognition.

Counselor: What do you say about Paul?

Fran: Well, executives could have them all.

Doris: They require a lot of education and aggressiveness.

Paul: Yeah, entertainment is aggressive, sort of. Not mean aggressive, just willing to get out and hustle and do your best.

Mary: And step on people to get on top.

Paul: No, I wouldn't hurt anyone; I am not competitive in a mean way, but fair.

Counselor:	So having these qualities is pointing out that you are competitive.
Fran:	I can tell that already.
Paul:	I know that, but it is not too important.
Counselor:	Should you have it on your list of work-relevant traits as something about a job that you would want to consider?
Paul:	I guess so. I like to compete some, and the job would not interest me if there weren't some challenges in it. At least a little competition.

SESSION 2: SHARING OCCUPATIONS

Steve:	My occupations are a credit manager, advertising manager, production manager, principal, engineer, and physician.
Counselor:	Do they say anything about you Steve?
Steve:	I don't think so, nothing in particular.
Fran:	They are all on top. I feel that you want to get to the top.
Paul:	Yeah. In all of them you tell others what to do. You're kind of a boss.
Counselor:	Does that sound like something important in a job—managing people?
Steve:	I like to. I like directing things and people. They usually go along. I'm not bad at it.
Counselor:	Great! That sounds like something that you really want to keep in mind.

SESSION 3: DECIDING ON NEEDED OCCUPATIONAL INFORMATION

Doris:	I don't know how much schooling hospital administrators need.

Paul:	Oh, they need a master's.
Counselor:	Asking people is a good information source, and it was good of you to volunteer that information Paul. Are there other ways Doris could find out about schooling required?
Doris:	I could look it up in that occupational book or ask someone.
Paul:	Yeah! Go down to the hospital and ask the admininstrators. They have to know.
Counselor:	Will you do that for next time?
Doris:	Well, I'll try, and if I can I'll find out more about the job because I only have a general idea about it.
Counselor:	Sounds like something worth doing. We'll expect you to tell us about your findings next time. O.K.?

SESSION 4:   REACTIONS TO DIFFERENCE SCORES

Counselor:	O.K. Barbara, suppose you tell us about your difference scores.
Barbara:	Well, they sound the most like dental hygienist, but I don't know.
Counselor:	You are not sure dental hygienist fits you?
Barbara:	No. I'd like dental hygienist, but I don't know if I could do it. I'm O.K. in biology, but I don't know.
Doris:	But you gotta try. If you put your mind to it, you could do it.
Steve:	When I try something it usually works out. You just gotta try.
Barbara:	Well, there is a lot of responsibility, and well, secretary is also close and I wouldn't mind working in an office. I would be with people.
Paul:	That would be less responsible.

Appendix F   121

Doris: Or maybe you could take a less responsible dental job.

Barbara: I don't know, secretary is all right, or maybe a receptionist.

Paul: Receptionist is easy, but it doesn't pay much. All you need is some typing. How well do you type?

Barbara: I'm doing O.K. in typing and steno.

Counselor: But getting back to dental hygienist, are you saying you wouldn't consider it because you don't feel confident?

Barbara: Well, it is a lot of responsibiilty. I don't know.

Fran: Yeah! Not feeling confident seems to fit you. You weren't confident in waitressing or in YWCA receptionist. Perhaps you could take a job helping people at a lower level, requiring less skill.

Doris: But you did O.K. in school and won't low confidence stop you in secretarial?

Fran: Yeah! That's right.

Barbara: O.K., O.K., you like helping people and you know you can do it, but even though I want to, I don't know I can. Like babysitting, I love kids but I lose patience when they scream. Kids are great but I don't want to traumatize them.

Doris: But you can learn patience. You can play games or read. Kids will behave.

Barbara: But I don't want to let anybody down. You know. Medical work is serious; you can't make mistakes.

Doris: You could change.

Barbara: I don't know. People don't change. I know lots of people who try to change and they don't.

Counselor: Doris and Fran are pointing out that your low esteem is preventing you from doing something

	you want to do. Maybe you could do something . . .
Barbara:	(low voice) I know.
Doris:	Yeah! Maybe you could go in at a lower level, and build up your confidence. Working with adults doesn't require that much patience. Even two or three would be enough.
Fran:	You have to try. You just can't give up.
Paul:	Yeah! That's important in business. Never give up.
Counselor:	Barbara?
Barbara:	Well . . . I'll try to find out more about the qualifications and think about it more. Maybe I could start lower and get confidence.
Doris:	I think you can do it.
Counselor:	Where will you get more information?
Barbara:	In that Occupational Outlook Book that Fran used.
Steve:	And you can talk to Mrs. Y. She teaches dental hygiene.
Counselor:	O.K. Suppose we talk about your thinking next time, Barbara, and see where you are. O.K.?
Barbara:	O.K.

SESSION 5: PROBLEM SOLVING

Counselor:	Last week Barbara was hesitating about dental hygienist because she lacked confidence. Lack of confidence was an obstacle to her goal. What are some alternatives for getting around that obstacle?
Barbara:	Well, I read more about it and talked to Mrs. Y. It didn't sound as hard as I thought, but I'm going Tuesday to watch a dental hygienist work. I think I will try it, though.

Counselor:	O.K. Barbara is using one alternative to tackling the obstacle. What is she doing?
Paul:	She is not worrying, and she is asking questions instead.
Counselor:	Good! She is getting more information to see whether she should be worried. Are there other ways she should attack the obstacle of low confidence?
Doris:	She could study and practice hard in training so she would be good, so she could build up her confidence.
Paul:	Yeah! She could start lower and work up to it like we said last time, or she could just relax and forget about it. You have to try things and not worry about how well you do. Before I do a show I'm scared, but I just do it and it works. You can't worry.
Counselor:	Good! You have given some alternate ways of handling confidence—to learn more about what is asked of you, to practice so you can improve, to start at a level you can handle, and to try your best without worrying.
Fran:	You could use them all. Yeah! They make sense.
Counselor:	Barbara, do you think that you will be able to use them?
Barbara:	I am going to try it out as a major. I do O.K. in school and I will work hard. I don't know if I can just stop worrying. I am not as worried—but everybody worries. It's helped thinking about what I'm going to do and getting more information. I think it will be O.K.
Steve & Doris:	You're right to try.

APPENDIX G

EXAMPLE OF A MASTER PLAN (WITH STUDY TIMES FILLED IN:)

TIME	MON.	TUES.	WED.	THURS.	FRI.	SAT.	SUN.
7-8	←―――――――― Dress and Breakfast ――――――――→						↑
8-9	History	Study Chem.	History	Study Chem.	History	↑	
9-10	Study History	Phy. Ed.	Study History	Phy. Ed.	Study History		
10-11	Study French	Chem.	Study French	Chem.	Study French	Work	
11-12	French	Study Chem.	French	Study Chem.	French	↓	
12-1	←―――――――――― Lunch ――――――――→						Free Time
1-2	Math.	Library	Math.	Library	Math.		
2-3	Study Math.	Theme	Study Math.		Study Math.		
3-4	Study English	Theme	Study English	Chem. Lab.	Study English		
4-5	English	Theme	English		English		
5-6	←―――――――― Recreation ――――――――→						↓

TIME	MON.	TUES.	WED.	THURS.	FRI.	SAT.	SUN.
6-7	←―――――――― Dinner ――――――――→					↑	Free time
7-8	Study English	Study Math.	Study English	Study Math.	Study English		English Theme
8-9	Study French	Study History	Study French	Study History	Study French	Free time or Review	English Theme
9-10	Review English	Review French	Review History	Reveiw Math.	Review Chem.		Study History
10-11	Recreational Reading						
11-12	Conversation, Sleep					↓	

APPENDIX G (Cont.)
Hot Sheet

Subject	Assignment	Estimated Time	Due Date	Time
History	150 pages	6½ hrs.	Wed.	8:00
English	Paper	12 hrs.	Mon.	4:00
Chemistry	20 pages—Read	4 hrs.	Thurs.	10:00
Math.	20 problems	6 hrs.	Fri.	1:00
French	Lesson 5	4 hrs.	Wed.	11:00

Daily Action Plan

Mon.	Read History: Start French:	9:30-10:30	3:30-6:00	1:00-10:00 10:00-11:00
Tues.	Read Chemistry: Finish French:		2:00-6:00	-: 7:00-10:00
Wed.	Do Math: Start English: —Paper—	9:30-10:30	3:30-5:30	-:: 7:00-11:00
Thurs.	Finish Math. English Paper: —Write—	2:00-5:00		::::-- 7:00-11:00
Fri.	English Paper: —Revise & Polish—	9:30-10:30		--::::
Sat.				
Sun.				

APPENDIX H

Excerpt from Bate's Time Management Counseling

Session 4, Sub-goals:
1. Have listed daily assignment times for week
2. Identify those who tried any part of the model
3. Identify blocks in sticking to their plan of action from last time

Phase I: *Review Time Plan Model and Previous Session*:

1   We've talked about three parts to the time plan model. The first part being a Master Plan or schedule which lists your fixed activities. The second part of the time plan model is your weekly Hot Sheet, where you have listed all of your weekly assignments and the third part, which we are starting to work on, is the bottom part of the Hot Sheet, your Daily Plan of Action. It is your plan for doing your daily assignments in an allotted amount of time. You look at the top part of the Hot Sheet, see you have a certain assignment with some estimate of how long it's going to take you to complete it, and then you look at your Master Plan and see when you can plan your daily time and list that time down here (*Point to the Bottom of the Hot Sheet*).

RULE: *Before Session, Leader Reviews Each Member's Written Plan of Action and Ask*:

2   What have you done between last Monday's session and today to follow the plan of action you set for yourself at the last session?
As Basis for Refreshing Their Memory, the Leader Can Use Their Written Plan of Action That They Were Going to Try Between Sessions. RULE: Try to Have Everyone Respond Without Going Around the Circle and Reinforce Those Who Give Positive Responses. Give Them Paper and Ask Them to Write Down the Answer to the Following Q's and Hand In:

3   1. Did you follow your plan basically or try any part of it at all?

4   2. Did you stick to any part of the Time Plan Model, i.e. the Master Plan, Hot Sheet—weekly assignments or daily plan of action?

5   3. Did you use it for a guide for one hour, one day or more than one day?

6   4. If you did not follow it at all, what was your reason for not following it?

7   5. If you made any modifications in it, what sort of modifications were necessary?

RULE: *Glance Over Their Responses as They Hand Them in and Ask Those Who Stuck to Their Action Plan*:

8   Do you feel differently as a result of carrying through your plan of action? What do you think are the reasons for feeling better or worse?

(One Q or other, or don't use if no one stuck to it)

BIBLIOGRAPHY

Adler, A.: *The Practice and Theory of Individual Psychology.* New York, Harcourt, 1927.

Alkin, M. C.: Products for improving educational evaluation. *Evaluation Comment* 2:3, 1970.

Anderson, E. C.: Promoting Career Information Seeking Through Group Counselor's Cues and Reinforcements. Unpublished doctoral dissertation, University of California, Los Angeles, 1970.

Aubrey, R. F. and Hosford, R. E.: Improving counseling skills. *Focus on Guidance,* 3:1-6 (6), 1971.

Ausubel, D. P.: A teaching strategy for culturally deprived students, in H. L. Miller and M. B. Smiley (Eds.): *Education for the Metropolis.* New York, Free Press, 1967.

Bandura, A.: *Principles of Behavior Modification.* New York, Holt, Rinehart & Winston, 1969.

Bates, J. C. and Sorenson, A. G.: Developing Repeatable Counseling Procedures. Unpublished paper, University of California, Los Angeles, 1973.

Bates, J. C.: Formative Evaluation in the Development of a Counseling Mode Designed to Teach Time Management. Unpublished doctoral dissertation, University of California, Los Angeles, 1971.

Bergin, A. E.: The evaluation of therapeutic outcomes. In Bergin, A. E. & Garfield, S. L. (Eds.): *Handbook of Psychotherapy and Behavior Change.* New York, Wiley, 1971.

Bergin, A. E. and Strupp, H. H.: New directions in psychotherapy research. *Journal of Abnormal Psychology,* 76: 1970.

Bingham, W.: Change of Occupations as a Function of the Regnancy of Self Concepts. Unpublished doctoral dissertation, Teachers College, Columbia University, 1967.

Birney, D., and others: *Life Planning Workshops: Discussion and Evaluation.* Fort Collins, Office of Student Development, Colorado State University, 1971.

Brayfield, A. H. and Crites, J. O.: Research on vocational guidance, in Borrow, H. (Ed.): *Man in a World at Work.* Boston, Houghton-Mifflin, 1964.

Campbell, D. P.: *Handbook for the Strong Vocational Interest Blank.* Stanford, Stanford University Press, 1971.

Campbell, D. P. and Stanley, J. C.: *Experimental and Quasi-experimental Designs for Research.* Chicago, Rand McNally & Co., 1963.

Campbell, R. E.: *Vocational Guidance: A Systems Approach*. Columbus, Center for Study of Vocational and Technical Education, Ohio State University. 1971.

Carkhuff, R.: *The Development of Human Resources*. New York, Holt, Rinehart, and Winston, 1971.

Carkhuff, R. R. and Berenson, B. G.: *Beyond Counseling and Therapy*. New York, Holt, Rinehart & Winston, 1967.

Carlson, R. E. and others: *The Measurement of Employment Satisfactoriness*. Minneapolis, Minnesota Studies in Vocational Rehabilitation, University of Minnesota, 1963.

Crites, J. O.: *The Career Maturity Inventory* (research edition). New York, CTB/McGraw Hill, 1973.

Crites, J. O.: *The Maturity of Vocational Attitudes in Adolescence*. Washington, American Personnel and Guidance Association, 1971.

Crites, J. O.: *Vocational Psychology*. New York, McGraw-Hill, 1969.

Crites, J. O.: Measurement of vocational maturity in adolescence: I. Attitude Test of the Vocational Development Inventory. *Psychological Monographs*, 72:595, 1965.

Danish, S. J. and others: The Self-help vocational decision making booklet. An unpublished booklet, Southern Illinois University, Carbondale, 1969.

Darcy, R. L.: *An Experimental Junior High School Course in Occupational Opportunities and Labor Market Processes*. Athens, Ohio University, 1968.

Farmer, H. S.: Formative Evaluation of an Instructional Model of Counseling. Unpublished doctoral dissertation, University of California, Los Angeles, 1970.

Farmer, J. A. and Williams, R. C.: An educational strategy for career change. *Adult Leadership*, 19:318-320, 1971.

Ford, D. H. and Urban, H. B.: Some historical and conceptual perspectives on psychotherapy and behavior change, in Bergin, A. E. and Garfield, S. L. (Eds.): *Handbook of Psychotherapy and Behavior Change*. New York, Wiley, 1971.

Fowler, R. D.: The current status of computer interpretation of psychological tests. *American Journal of Psychiatry*, 125:21-27, 1969.

Gagnè, R. M.: *The Conditions of Learning*. New York, Holt, Rinehart, Winston, 1965.

Ghiselli, E. E.: *The Self-Description Inventory*. Unpublished test, University of California, Berkeley, 1971.

Ginzberg, E.: Toward a theory of occupational choice: a restatement. *Vocational Guidance Quarterly*, 20:169-176, 1972.

Ginzberg, E. and others: *Occupational Choice: An Approach to a General Theory*. New York, Columbia University Press, 1951.

Graff, R. W., Danish, S. and Austin, B.: Reactions to three kinds of vocational-educational counseling. *Journal of Counseling Psychology*, 19:224-228, 1972.

Gribbons, W. D. and Lohnes, P. R.: *Emerging Careers: A Study of 111 Adolescents.* New York, Teachers College Press, 1968.

Grummon, D. T.: Client-centered theory, in B. Stefflre and W. H. Grant, (Eds.): *Theories of Counseling* (2nd Ed.). New York, McGraw-Hill, 1972.

Guilford, J. P.: *Personality.* New York, McGraw-Hill, 1959.

Harren, U. A.: The vocational decision making process among college males. *Journal of Counseling Psychology, 13*:271-277, 1966.

Harren, V. A.: *Preliminary Manual for Vocational Decision Making Checklist.* Carbondale, University of Southern Illinois, 1972.

Healy, C. C.: Relation of occupational choice to the similarity between self-ratings and occupational ratings. *Journal of Counseling Psychology, 15*:317-323, 1968.

Healy, C. C.: The relation of esteem and social class to self-occupational congruence. *Journal of Vocational Behavior, 3*:43-53, 1973.

Healy, C. C.: A replicable method of group career counseling. *Vocational Guidance Quarterly, 21*:214-221, 1973.

Healy, C. C., Bailey, M. L., and Anderson, E. C.: The relation of esteem and vocational counseling to range of incorporation scores. *Journal of Vocational Behavior, 3*:69-75, 1973.

Healy. C. C. and Klein, S. P.: *The New Mexico Career Education Test Series.* Hollywood, California, Monitor, P.O. Box 2337, 1973.

Hershenson, D. B.: Occupational Plans Questionnaire. Unpublished test, Illinois Institute of Technology, undated.

Hewer, J.: Group counseling, individual counseling, and a college class in vocations. *Personal and Guidance Journal, 37*:660-665, 1959.

Hewer, V. H.: Evaluation of a criterion: Realism of vocational choice. *Journal of Counseling Psychology, 13*:289-294, 1966.

Hewer, V.: Group counseling. *Vocational Guidance Quarterly, 16*:250-257, 1968.

Hoffnung, R. J. and Mills, R. B.: Situational group counseling with disadvantaged youth. *Personnel and Guidance Journal, 48*:458-464, 1970.

Holland, J. L.: A theory of vocational choice. *Journal of Counseling Psychology, 6*:35-45, 1959.

Holland, J.: *Vocational choice.* Waltham, Waltham Press, 1966.

Holland, J. L. and others: A psychological classification of occupations. *Journal Supplement Abstract Service, 2*:84-85, 1972.

Ivey, A.: *Microcounseling: Innovations in Interviewing Training.* Springfield, Charles C Thomas, 1971.

Kagen, N.: *Interpersonal Process Recall: Training Model Recorded on Videotape.* E. Lansing, Michigan State University, 1972.

Kaple, D. J. and Kaple, M. K.: *Special Counseling for the Disadvantaged Adult.* Englewood Cliffs, Prentice Hall, 1972.

Katz, M. R.: Can computers make guidance decisions for students? *College Board Review,* 72:13-17, 1969.
Kelly, E. L. and Fiske, D. W.: *The Prediction of Performance in Clinical Psychology.* Ann Arbor, University of Michigan Press, 1951.
Korman, A. K.: Self-esteem variable in vocational choice. *Journal of Applied Psychology,* 50:479-486, 1966.
Korman, A. K.: Perceived abilities and vocational choice. *Journal of Applied Psychology,* 51:65-67, 1967.
Korman, A. K.: Self-esteem as a moderator in vocational choice: replications and extension. *Journal of Applied Psychology,* 53:188-193, 1969.
Korman, A. K.: Toward an hypothesis of work behavior. *Journal of Applied Psychology,* 54:31-41, 1970.
Krumboltz, J. D. and Schroeder, W. W.: Promoting career planning through reinforcement. *Personnel and Guidance Journal,* 44:19-26, 1965.
Krumboltz, J. D. and Thoresen, C. E. (Eds.): *Behavioral Counseling.* New York, Holt, Rinehart & Winston, 1969.
Krumboltz, J. D. and Thoresen, C. E.: The effect of behavioral counseling in group and individual settings on information-seeking behavior. *Journal of Counseling Psychology,* 11:324-333, 1964.
Krumboltz, J. D., Varenhorst, B. and Thoresen, C. E.: Non-verbal factors in effectiveness of models in counseling. *Journal of Counseling Psychology,* 14:412-418, 1967.
Kuder, G. F.: *Occupational Interest Survey.* Chicago, Science Research Associates, 1966.
Kuder, G. F.: *Vocational Preference Inventory, Form C.* Chicago, Science Research Associates, 1948.
London, P.: *The Modes and Morals of Psychotherapy.* New York, Holt, Rinehart & Winston, 1964.
Magoon, T.: Developing skills for educational and vocational counseling. In Krumboltz, J. D. and Thoresen, C. E. (Eds.): *Behavioral Counseling: Cases and Techniques.* New York, Holt, Rinehart & Winston, 1969.
Mannis, L. G. and Mochizuki, J.: Search for fulfillment: A program for adult women. *Personnel and Guidance Journal,* 50:594-599, 1972.
Marsden, G.: Content analysis studies of psychotherapy. In Bergin, A. E. and Garfield, S. L. (Eds.): *Handbook of Psychotherapy and Behavior Change.* New York, Wiley, 1971.
Mischel, W.: *Introduction to Personality.* New York, Holt, Rinehart & Winston, 1971.
Moreno, J. L. (Ed.): *The International Handbook of Group Psychotherapy.* New York, Philosophical Library, 1964.
Morrill, W. and Forest, D. J.: Dimensions of counseling for career development. *Personnel and Guidance Journal,* 49:299-307, 1970.
O'Connell, T. J. and Sedlacek, W. E.: The reliability of Holland's Self Directed Search for Educational and Vocational Planning. Research Report 6-71, Counseling Center, University of Maryland, 1971.

Osipow, S. H.: *Theories of Career Development.* New York, Appleton-Century-Crofts, 1968.
Osipow, S. H. and Walsh, W. B.: *Strategies in Counseling for Behavior Change.* New York, Appleton-Century-Crofts, 1970.
Otto, H. A.: *Human Potentialities: The Challenge and the Promise.* St. Louis, W. H. Green, 1968.
Otto, H.: Multiple strength perception method, Minerva Experience, and others. In Otto, H. (Ed.): *Explorations in Human Potential.* Springfield, Thomas, 1966.
Oppenheimer, E. A.: The relationship between certain self construct and occupational preferences. *Journal of Counseling Psychology, 13*:191-197, 1966.
Patterson, C. H. (Ed.): *Theories of Counseling and Psychotherapy.* New York, Harper & Row, 1966.
Patterson, C. H.: Counseling: Self-clarification and the helping relationship. In Borow, H. (Ed.): *Man in a World at Work.* Boston, Houghton-Mifflin, 1964.
Pauk, W.: *How to Study in College.* Boston, Houghton Mifflin, 1957.
Pruzak, J. A.: Learning job-seeking interview skills. In Krumboltz, J. D. and Thoresen, C. E. (Eds.): *Behavioral Counseling Cases and Techniques.* New York, Holt, Rinehart & Winston, 1969.
Quinn, J. B.: The influence of interpersonal perception on the process of change in two experimental modes of group process. Unpublished doctoral dissertation, University of California, Los Angeles, 1970.
Robinson, F. P.: *Effective Study.* New York, Harper & Row, 1946.
Rogers, C. R. and Dymond, R. F. (Eds.): *Psychotherapy and Personality Change: Coordinated Research Studies in the Client-centered Approach.* Chicago, University of Chicago Press, 1954.
Rogers, C. R. (Ed.): *The Therapeutic Relationship and Its Impact.* Madison, University of Wisconsin Press, 1967.
Rogers, C. R.: *On Becoming a Person: A Therapist's View of Psychotherapy.* Boston, Houghton-Mifflin, 1961.
Rogers, C. R.: *Client-centered Therapy.* Boston, Houghton-Mifflin, 1951.
Rotter, J. B.: Generalized expectancies for internal vs. external control of reinforcement. *Psychological Monographs, 80*:1, 1966.
Roueche, J. E.: Guidance and counseling. *ERIC UCLA Junior College Research Review, 3*: Sept., 1968.
Ryan, A. T.: *Effect of an Integrated Instructional Counseling Program to Improve Vocational Decision Making.* Washington, U.S. Department of Health, Education & Welfare, Project No. HRD 413-655-0154, 1968.
Samler, J.: Occupational exploration in counseling: A proposed reorientation. In Borow, H. (Ed.): *Man in a World at Work.* Boston, Houghton-Mifflin, 1964.
Shartle, R.: *Occupational Information.* New Jersey, Prentice Hall. 1959.
Sherwood, J. J.: Self-report and projective measures of achievement and affiliation. *Journal of Consulting Psychology, 30*:329-337, 1966.

Shiner, E. V.: Self-concept and Change of Occupation. Unpublished doctoral dissertation, Teachers College, Columbia University, 1963.

Shostrom, E. L.: *Personal Orientation Inventory.* San Diego, Educational and Industrial Testing Service, 1962.

Slocum, J. W. and Hand, H. H.: A longitudinal study of the effects of a human relations training program on managerial effectiveness. *Journal of Applied Psychology, 36*:412-417, 1972.

Sorenson, A. G.: Evaluation for the improvement of instructional programs: Some practical steps. *UCLA Center for the Study of Evaluation: Evaluation Comment, 2*:13-17. 1971.

Sorenson, A. G.: *Toward an Instructional Model for Counseling.* Los Angeles, Center for the Study of Evaluation, University of California, 1967.

Sorenson, A. G.: Pterodactyls, passenger pigeons, and personnel workers. *Personnel and Guidance Journal, 43*:430-438, 1964.

Sorenson, A. G. and Hawkins, R.: *Three Experimental Modes of Counseling.* Los Angeles, Center for the Study of Evaluation. University of California, 1968.

Sprague, D. G. and Strong, D. J.: Vocational choice group counseling. *Journal of College Student Personnel, 15*:35-45, 1970.

Strong, E. K.: *The Strong Vocational Interest Blank.* Palo Alto, Stanford University Press, 1927.

Strong, E. K.: *Vocational Interests 18 Years After College.* Minneapolis, University of Minnesota Press, 1955.

Sullivan, H. S.: *The Psychiatric Interview.* New York, Norton & Co., 1953.

Sullivan, H. S.: *The Interpersonal Theory of Psychiatry.* New York, Norton & Co., 1953.

Super, D. E.: Vocational development theory in 1988: How will it come about? *Counseling Psychologist, 1*:9-14, 1969.

Super, D. E.: *Career Development: Self-concept theory.* New York, College Entrance Board, Research Monograph No. 4, 1963.

Super, D. E. and others: *The Vocational Maturity of 9th Graders.* New York, Columbia University Press, 1960.

Super, D. E.: *The Psychology of Careers.* New York, Harper & Row, 1957.

Super, D. E.: A theory of career development. *American Psychologist, 8*:185-190, 1953.

Super, D. E.: *Appraising Vocational Fitness.* New York, Harper & Row, 1949.

Super, D. E. and others: *Vocational Development: A Framework for Research.* New York, Teachers College Press, Columbia University, 1957.

Super, D. E. and Jordaan, J. P.: *Career Development Theory.* Unpublished Paper, career pattern study in Teachers College, Columbia University, 1972.

Super, D. E.: *Career Development Inventory, Form 1.* New York, Teachers College Press, Columbia University, 1971.

Super, D. E., Kowalski, R. S. and Gotkin, E. H.: *Floundering and Trial After High School.* New York, Teachers College Press, Columbia University, 1969.

Thorensen, C. E.: Relevance and research in counseling. *Review of Educational Research, 32*:263-281, 1969.

Tiedeman, D. V. and O'Hara, R. P.: *Career Development: Choice and Integration.* New York, College Entrance Board, 1963.

Tiedeman, D. V. and O'Hara, R. P.: Vocational self concept in adolescence. *Journal of Counseling Psychology, 6*:292-301, 1959.

Toffler, A.: *Future Shock.* New York, Random House, 1970.

Truax, C. R.: Reinforcement and nonreinforcement in Rogerian psychotherapy. *Journal of Abnormal Psychology, 71*:1-9, 1966.

Trueblood, R. W. and McHolland, J. D.: *Self-actualization and the Human Potential Group Process.* Evanston, Counseling Center, Kendall College, undated.

Tyler, L.: *The Work of the Counselor.* New York, Appleton-Century-Crofts, 1969.

Vivell, S.: Evaluation of a Counseling Program for Teaching Time Management. Unpublished M.A. thesis, University of California, Los Angeles, 1972.

Vriend, J.: Vocational maturity ratings of inner-city high school seniors. *Journal of Counseling Psychology, 16*:377-384, 1969.

Whitely, J. M.: *Research in Counseling: Evaluation and Refocus.* Columbus, Merrill, 1967.

Whitney, D.: Predicting from expressed vocational choice: A review. *Personnel and Guidance Journal, 48*:279-286, 1970.

Williamson, E. G.: *How to Counsel Students: A Manual of Techniques for Clinical Counselors.* New York, McGraw-Hill. 1939.

Williamson, E. G.: *Counseling Adolescents.* New York, McGraw-Hill, 1949.

Women's Career Information Test. Columbus, Center for the Study of Vocational and Technical Education, Ohio State University, 1970.

Wylie, Ruth C.: *The Self-Concept.* Lincoln, University of Nebraska Press, 1961.

Zenner, T. B. and Schnuelle, L.: *An Evaluation of the Self-Directed Search.* Baltimore, Report 124, Center for Social Organization of Schools. Johns Hopkins University, 1972.

INDEX

A

Ability to solve career problems, 82
Acceptance of responsibility for
  planning, viii, 80
Accountability, 73
Adler, A., 42
Adult changing occupations, 39
Agent
  role of, 67, 71
Anderson, B., 43
Anderson, E. C., 23
Appraisal
  in Effective Problem Solving
    counseling, 34
  in reinforcement and simulation
    reinforcement counseling, 19
  in System of Interaction, Guidance,
    and Information, 36
  in trait factor counseling, 15, 18
  in vocational choice case study
    counseling, 32
Atmosphere
  in counseling, 3, 73
  its establishment by Rogers, 40-41
  its establishment by Ryan, 19
Attitude
  about career, 82
  about information seeking, 77
Aubrey, R. F., x
Austin, B., 35
Ausubel, D. P., 7, 39

B

Bandura, A., x, 50, 63
Bates, J. C., 11, 38, 56-60, 67, 74-75
Berenson, B. G., 43
Bergin, A. E., viii
Bingham, W., 29

Birney, D., 48
Blum, Z. D., 61
Brayfield, A., viii

C

Cabrillo College, 86
Campbell, D. P., 32
Campbell, R. E., 75
Career Counseling Procedures
  client-centered counseling, 40-43
  discovery (consciousness raising)
    procedures, 43-50
  Effective Problem Solving, 51-53
  guided inquiry, 50-55
  human potential, 43-46
  life planning workshops, 46-50
  placement skills, 62-64
  reinforcement counseling, 18-24,
    87-96
  self-concept counseling, 24-30,
    114-122
  Self Directed Search, 60-62
  simulation-reinforcement, 18-24,
    96-113
  System of Interaction, Information
    and Guidance, 36
  time management, 55-60, 123-125
  trait-factor, 13-18
  vocational choice case study, 30-33
Career development
  methods of assessing, 75-85
  of adults changing occupations, 39
  of homemakers, 39
  of the disadvantaged, 39
  tests of
    Career Development Inventory,
      77-78
    Career Maturity Inventory, 78-82
    New Mexico Career Development
      Test, 77-82

Vocational Decision Making
   Checklist, 83
Women's Career Information
   Test, 78-83
Career Development Inventory, 77-78
Career information
   attitude about obtaining, 77
   contacts with sources of, 77
   dissemination in client-centered
      counseling, 42
   extent of, 77
   knowledge of sources of, 77
Career Maturity Inventory, 78-82
Career planning
   as common goal of counseling
      procedures, 12
   completeness of, 80
   emphasis on in 13 procedures, 67-68
   extent of, 80
   for fictitious person, 24
   knowledge about, 79-80
   on basis of tests and inventories,
      67-68
   realism of, 81
   responsibility for, 80
Career Planning Program, 27
Career Pattern Study, 78-80
Career skills, 83
Carkhuff, R., ix-x, 43
Carlson, R. E., 84
Case study
   of a simulated person, 22-24, 96-98
   presenting one's own, 30-32
Client-centered counseling, 40-43,
   73-74
Client reactions, classification of, 6
Client role in group counseling, 9
Community colleges
   Blue Mountain Community College,
      16, 17
   Cabrillo College, 17, 86
   Des Moines Area Community
      College, 39
   Mercer County College, 36
   Modesto Junior College, 39
   Phoenix College, 49
   Santa Monica College, 29

Suffolk County Community College,
   17
Ulster Community College, 39, 44
Computer-assisted counseling
   in trait factor counseling, 18
   SIGI, 36
Contacts with informational sources,
   77
Counseling (*see also* Replicable
   counseling)
   and examined life, 67
   and systematic planning, 68
   classification of client reactions in, 6
   classification of counselor responses
      in, 6-7
   criteria or indices of, 8
   evaluation of the process of, 73
   methods of learning, ix
   rules of, 6
Crites, J. O., viii, 78-85
Cue questions
   in Ryan's counseling procedures, 19
   in Sorenson's guided inquiry, 50

D

Danish, S. J., 35
Darcy, R. C., 78
Dawis, R. V., 84
Decision making (*see* Career planning,
   Planning, and Problem solving)
Deliberation
   as common element of counseling, 65
   in guided inquiry counseling, 50
   modeled by Williamson, 14
Developing hypotheses, stage of trait
   factor counseling, 14
Developmental tasks
   defined by Super and Ginzberg, ix
   of adults, disadvantaged and
      homemakers, 39
Diagnosis, 6, 14
Difference scores, in Healy's procedure,
   27
Disadvantaged
   developmental tasks of, 39
   helped by human potential
      counseling, 44

Index

helped by reinforcement counseling, 18
Discovery group counseling, 43-50
Discovery learning, 51
Discussion of values, 46
Distributed study, 58
Dymond, R. F., 79

E

Effective Problem Solving, 51-53
England, G. W., 84
Evaluation
   during counseling, 67
   of counseling outcomes, 75-85
   of counseling process, 73-74
   of differences among career counseling procedures, 67-68
Execution of career plan, 67, 71, 82
Extent of educational, occupational and manpower information, 77-78
Extent of planning, 80

F

Farmer, H. S., 55
Farmer, J. A., 40
Fiske, D. W., 13
Follow-up
   in guided inquiry counseling, 54
   in 13 counseling procedures, 68
   in trait-factor counseling, 16
Forest, D. J., viii
Fowler, R. D., 18

G

Gagné, E. M., 7, 55, 59
Gensler, S. A., 35
Ghiselli, E. E., 79
Ginsberg, E., ix, 79
Goal setting
   exercise in life planning workshop, 48
   requirements for, 44
   specificity in different counseling procedures, 67

Graff, R. W., 35
Gribbons, W. D., 78-81
Group Counseling
   client roles, 9
   guidelines at Modesto Community College, 43
   implications of replicability for, 9-10
Grummon, D. T., 42
Guided inquiry counseling, 50-55

H

Hand, H. H., 71
Harren, V. A., 83
Hawkins, R., 55
Healy, C. C., 43, 67, 74-79
   self-concept counseling, 12, 24-30, 114-122
Hershenson, D. D., 80
Hewer, V. H., 13, 31-33, 81
Hinkle, J. E., 48
Hoffnung, R. J., 71
Holland, J. L., 26, 38, 60-62
Homemaker, career development tasks of, 39
   helped by discovery group counseling, 49
Hosford, R. E., x
Hot sheet, 56, 124
Human potential counseling, 43-46
Hypothesis dissemenation in trait factor counseling, 15-16

I

Identification and stripping of roles exercise, 47
Inception phase of trait factor counseling, 14
Information processing, criteria of, 76-78
Input of concerned others to career planning, 71
Ivey, A., ix

J

Job seeking knowledge, 84
Junior colleges (*see* Community Colleges)

K

Kagen, N., ix
Kaple, D. J., 71
Kaple, M. K., 71
Karwert, N. L., 61
Kass, E., 49
Katz, M. R., 36
Kelley, E. L., 13
Klein, S. P., 77-83
Knowledge about career planning, 79
Knowledge of informational sources, 77
Korman, A. K., 42, 49
Krumboltz, J. D., 13. 33, 77
Kuder Occupational Interest Survey, 32
Kuder Preference Inventory, 60
Kuo, H., 61

L

Level of test interpretation
  in EPS, 35
  in vocational choice case study counseling, 32
Life inventory exercise, 47
Life line exercise, 46-47
Life planning workshops, 46-48
Limitations among career counseling procedures, 68
Lofquist, L. H., 84
Lohnes, P. R., 78-81
London, P., 55

M

Magoon, T., 12, 33-35
Mannis, L. G., 49
Marsden, G., 73
Master time plan, 56, 123
McHolland, J. D., 46-48

Mills, R. D., 71
Mischel, W., 78
Mochizuki, J., 49
Modeling
  an aid to replicability, 49
  in client-centered counseling, 40
  in guided inquiry counseling, 50
  in trait-factor counseling, 14
  of peers, 67-68
Morrill, W., viii
Myers, R. A., 78

N

New Mexico Career Education Test Series, 77-82
News release exercise, 47

O

Occupation
  satisfaction with, 84
  satisfactory performance of, 84
Occupational
  areas, Holland's six, 25, 115
  information, extent of, 77
  rating, 25
O'Connell, T. J., 62
O'Hara, R. P., 79, 83
Oppenheimer, E. A., 79
Osipow, S. H., 13
Otto, H. A., 44-46, 48

P

Parsons, F., xii, 13
Patterson, C. H., 8, 42
Pauk, W., 59
Personality type, 88
Placement skills procedures, 92
Planning
  acceptance of responsibility for, 112
  based on tests and inventories, 97
  career, 107 (*see* Career planning)
  completeness of, 114

criteria of, 107
extent of, 111
phase in trait-factor counseling, 26-27
realism of, 113
steps of, 43-44
systematic, 97
teaching by simulation, 97
time, 82
vocational, 109
Plan of action, 83
Problem Solving
ability for career, 82
class of counselor responses, 6-7
limited number of methods, 70
phases of, in guided inquiry, 51
steps in, 28
stimulating it through unplanned events, 23
Pruzak, J. A., 63

Q

Quinn, J. B., 55
Quirck, J., 44-46

R

Readiness for Vocational Planning, 78-81
Reassume roles exercise, 71
Reconnaissance phase of trait factor counseling, 14
Reinforcement counseling, 18-24, 87-96
Replicability
and accountability, viii
and eclecticism, 10
as a characteristic of counseling, 1-9
Replicable counseling, 3-11
Responsibility for implementing counseling plan, 96
Robinson, F. P., 55, 59
Rogers, C. R., 7, 8, 38, 40-43, 67, 73, 74, 79
Role
of agent, 67, 70
of client in group counseling, 9
playing, 62-64
reversal, 63
Rotter, J. B., 71
Rules of counseling, 12
Ryan, A., 12, 18-24, 37, 87-113

S

Samler, J., 17
Satisfaction with occupation, 85
satisfactory vocational performance, 85
Schnuelle, L., 62
Schroeder, W. W., 77
Sedlacek, W. E., 61
Self
acceptance or esteem, 66-67, 79
accuracy of knowledge about, 79
methods of knowing, 27
rating, 27
Self Directed Search, 60-62
Shartle, R., 55, 84
Sherwood, J. J., 78
Shiner, E. V., 29
Simulation reinforcement counseling, 18-24, 96-113
Slocum, J. W., 71
Sorenson, A. G., x, 11, 50-55, 67, 83
Sprague, D. G., 31-33
Stanley, J. C., 75
Strength bombardment, 68
Strong, E. K., 29
Study skills program, 60
Success bombardment, 69
Sullivan, H. S., 14, 17, 42
Super, D. E., ix, 13, 29, 76-84

T

Task analysis, 85
Thomas, L. E., 48
Thoresen, C. E., 13, 35, 76-77
Tiedeman, D. V., 79, 83

Time management counseling, 55-60, 123-125
Toffler, A., 76
Training programs in counseling techniques, 4
Trait-factor counseling, 13-18
Truax, C. R., 7, 42-43
Trueblood, R. W., 44, 48
Tyler, L., 13, 17, 76
Typical and special day of future exercise, 71

V

Values, discussion of, 69
Verbal cues, 31
Viernstein, M. C., 61
Vivell, S., 60, 75
Vocational choice case study, 30-33
Vocational decision making checklist, 83
Vocational development, 77-79
Vocational planning (*see* Planning)
Vocational satisfactoriness, 85
Vocational success, 85
Vriend, J., 78

W

Walsh, W. B., 13
Whiteley, J. M., viii
Whitney, D., 81
Williamson, E. G., vii, 8, 12-17, 37, 66-67
Williams, R. C., 40
Women's Career Information Test, 78, 83
Work-relevant qualities, 40
Wylie, R. C., 79

Z

Zenner, T. B., 62